FOOD PROCESSOR COOKBOOK

for Beginners

Delicious Dishes Made Faster with Your Kitchen Gadget

- Maricela D. West -

©Copyright 2024 All rights reserved

TABLE OF CONTENT

INTRODUCTION 6
GETTING STARTED WITH YOUR FOOD PROCESSOR 7
ESSENTIAL TECHNIQUES AND TIPS 7

Blueberry Smoothie 8	Almond Butter Yogurt 25
Classic Guacamole 8	Coconut Macaroons 25
Cherry Compote 8	Gingerbread Macaroons 25
Orange Macaroons 9	Cheesy Spinach Dip 25
Spinach Fritters 9	Spicy Salsa 26
Sweet Potato Fritters 9	Mango Smoothie 26
Cilantro Lime Rice 10	Flaxseed Energy Balls 26
Fruit Compote 10	Agave Yogurt 26
Pistachio Cheese 11	Maple Energy Balls 26
Pistachio Milk Yogurt 11	Oatmeal Raisin Cookies 27
Guacamole Dip 11	Pineapple Smoothie 27
Greek Yogurt Dip 12	Vegan Mozzarella 27
Queso Dip 12	Mint Macaroons 28
Smoked Salmon Dip 12	Green Goddess Dip 28
Broccoli Fritters 13	Classic Hummus 28
Red Velvet Energy Balls 13	Split Pea Soup 28
S'mores Energy Balls 13	Shortbread Cookies 29
Cashew Milk Smoothie 14	Almond Macaroons 29
Gingerbread Cookies 14	Chocolate Butter 29
Vanilla Energy Balls 14	Raspberry Smoothie 29
Creamy Avocado Dip 15	Citrus Herb Spread 30
Pumpkin Seed Energy Balls 15	Cream of Broccoli Soup 30
Raspberry Energy Balls 15	Sugar Cookies 30
Flaxseed Cheese 15	Spicy Vegan Chees 31
Protein Energy Balls 16	Fresh Basil Pesto 31
Spicy Garlic Herb Rub 16	Oatmeal Smoothie 31
Crab Rangoon Dip 16	Hazelnut Spread 31
Beet Fritters 16	Garlic Mashed Cauliflower 32
Hummus Dip 17	Beet Soup 32
Blue Cheese Dip 17	Citrus Compote 32
Nutella 17	Corn Fritters 32
Quinoa Energy Balls 18	Lemon Garlic Aioli 33
Peanut Butter Energy Balls 18	Flax Milk Yogurt 33
Pumpkin Spice Compote 18	Almond Energy Balls 33
Chipotle Dip 19	Soy Milk Cheese 33
Smoothie Base 19	Safflower Cheese 34
Cranberry Compote 19	Creamy Avocado Dressing 34
Honey Butter 19	Soy Milk Yogurt 34
Oatmeal Energy Balls 20	Spinach Artichoke Dip 34
Quinoa Burgers 20	Fresh Herb Butter 35
Ginger Pear Compote 20	Creamy Salsa Verde 35
Green Smoothie 21	Creamy Cauliflower Sauce 35
Nut Butter Energy Balls 21	Spinach Soup 36
Cherry Smoothie 21	Mint Chocolate Energy Balls.............. 36
Macadamia Nut Cheese 21	Veggie Fritters 36
Vegan Goat Cheese 22	Strawberry Energy Balls 37
Brownie Energy Balls 22	Peanut Butter Spread 37
Cashew Chocolate Spread 22	Berry Smoothie 37
White Chocolate Macadamia Cookies ... 22	Pecan Butter 37
Snickerdoodle Cookies 23	Pistachio Energy Balls 38
Latkes 23	Mango Salsa 38
Vegan Mascarpone 24	Pumpkin Pie Energy Balls 38
Minestrone 24	Fermented Nut Cheese 38
Peach Compote 24	Cinnamon Butter 39

Recipe	Page
Vegetable Soup	39
Carrot Fritters	39
Sun-Dried Tomato Spread	40
Vegan Cream Cheese	40
Artichoke Parmesan Dip	40
Macadamia Nut Butter	40
Chia Seed Energy Balls	41
Asparagus Soup	41
Coconut Milk Cheese	41
Strawberry Chocolate Spread	42
Cashew Cheese	42
Gazpacho	42
Creamy Tomato Soup	42
Protein Smoothie	43
Artichoke Spread	43
Cinnamon Energy Balls	43
Blueberry Energy Balls	43
Blueberry Lemon Spread	44
Lentil Patties	44
Banana Lentil Patties	44
Banana Oat Cookies	45
Hash Browns	45
Vegan Feta	45
Maple Syrup Yogurt	46
Caramel Spread	46
Mocha Energy Balls	46
Chia Seed Jam	46
Vegan Cheese Spread	47
Roasted Pepper Spread	47
Thai Peanut Dip	47
Honey Yogurt	47
Coconut Energy Balls	47
Kale Smoothie	48
Cauliflower Soup	48
Blueberry Macaroons	48
Vegan Gouda	48
Nutella Copycat Spread	49
Vanilla Smoothie	49
Almond Joy Macaroons	49
Mixed Fruit Compote	50
Chocolate Energy Balls	50
Chocolate Almond Spread	50
Vanilla Yogurt	50
Chocolate Macaroons	51
Chocolate Crinkle Cookies	51
Walnut Energy Balls	51
Blackberry Energy Balls	52
Sesame Seed Energy Balls	52
Peanut Butter Banana Smoothie	52
Simple Pesto Sauce	52
Matcha Energy Balls	53
Chipotle Lime Vinaigrette	53
Plum Compote	53
Cookies with Chocolate Chips	53
Berry Compote	54
Spiced Fruit Compote	54
Herb Butter	54
Italian Herb Spread	55
Chocolate Hazelnut Spread	55
Spiced Pumpkin Soup	55
Sweet and Sour Sauce	55
Rice Milk Cheese	56
Almond Butter Smoothie	56
Pumpkin Spice Spread	56
Mint Chocolate Spread	56
Cauliflower Fritters	57
Cashew Parmesan	57
Brazilian Nut Cheese	57
Baba Ganoush	57
Sunflower Seed Energy Balls	58
Caramelized Onion Dip	58
Roasted Red Pepper Dip	58
Carrot Ginger Soup	58
Cinnamon Roll Energy Balls	59
Lemon Macaroons	59
Cookie Dough Energy Balls	59
White Chocolate Spread	60
Potato Pancakes	60
Rice Milk Yogurt	60
Thai Peanut Sauce	60
Garlic Butter	60
Almond Chocolate Spread	61
Pistachio Butter	61
Cashew Milk Yogurt	61
French Onion Dip	61
Mushroom Soup	62
Maple Pecan Spread	62
Cashew Energy Balls	62
Hemp Milk Yogurt	62
Roasted Red Pepper Sauce	63
Artichoke Dip	63
Macadamia Nut Cookies	63
Ginger Energy Balls	63
Apple Cinnamon Spread	64
Hemp Seed Energy Balls	64
Sweet Potato Soup	64
Pear Compote	64
Lentil Soup	65
Vegetable Soup Base	65
+Potato Leek Soup	65
Almond Joy Energy Balls	65
Creamed Spinach	66
Maple Butter	66
Olive Tapenade	66
Vegan Mayonnaise	66
Quick Salsa	67
Cinnamon Macaroons	67
Spinach Spread	67
Vanilla Macaroons	68
Sweet Vegan Cheese	68
Compound Butter	68
Date Spread	68
Pimento Cheese	69
Pecan Energy Balls	69
Cinnamon Sugar Spread	69
Black Bean Burgers	69
Coconut Almond Energy Balls	70
Chia Seed Cheese	70
Almond Milk Yogurt	70
Pecan Sandies	70
Honey Walnut Spread	71
Nut and Seed Granola	71

Sunflower Seed Cheese	71
Olive Spread	71
Vegan Cheddar	72
Black Bean Dip	72
Mediterranean Spread	72
Coffee Energy Balls	72
Apple Cinnamon Energy Balls	73
Sun-Dried Tomato Dip	73
Lemon Energy Balls	73
Pumpkin Spice Macaroons	74
Homemade Nut Butter	74
Greek Tzatziki	74
Strawberry Macaroons	75
Almond Cookies	75
Macadamia Energy Balls	75
Smoky Vegan Cheese	75
Lemon Herb Butter	76
Red Velvet Macaroons	76
Apple Compote	76
Falafel	76
Strawberry Banana Smoothie	77
Banana Compote	77
Carrot Soup	78
Veggie Burgers	78
Raspberry Macaroons	78
Chocolate Hazelnut Energy Balls	78
Chocolate Chip Energy Balls	79
Avocado Smoothie	79
Oat Milk Yogurt	79
Peanut Butter Cookies	79
Apple Cinnamon Oatmeal	80
Chocolate Yogurt	80
Mango Compote	80
Buffalo Chicken Dip	81
Sweet Potato Hummus	81
Pistachio Macaroons	81
Chocolate Smoothie	81
Sweet Corn Soup	82
Coconut Chocolate Macaroons	82
Macadamia Nut Milk Yogurt	82
Tahini Energy Balls	83
Spinach Smoothie	83
Birthday Cake Energy Balls	83
Tomato Soup	83
Vegan Blue Cheese	84
Peanut Butter Yogurt	84
Tofu Cream Cheese	84
Apricot Compote	85
Mocha Macaroons	85
Homemade Refried Beans	85
Lemon Poppy Seed Macaroons	85
Fresh Tomato Sauce	86
Pineapple Compote	86
Raspberry Vanilla Spread	86
Pumpkin Seed Cheese	86
Walnut Butter	87
Chickpea Burgers	87
Vegan Paneer	87
Tahini Cheese	87
Almond Ricotta	88
Almond Flour Pancakes	88
Lemon Poppy Seed Energy Balls	88
Easy Falafel	88
Cookies and Cream Macaroons	89
Salted Caramel Energy Balls	89
Mango Macaroons	89
Vegetable Dip	90
Classic Salsa	90
Butternut Squash Soup	90
Pistachio Spread	91
THE END	92

INTRODUCTION

You have entered the realm of food processors. Prepare to be amazed if you've never used this multipurpose cooking gadget before. You won't find a more versatile and powerful kitchen device than a food processor. Making quick work of meal preparation and opening up a world of new culinary possibilities, it can chop, slice, combine, and puree just about anything.

Everything you need to know about using a food processor, from proper setup to the function of each attachment and how to maintain it clean and in excellent working order is covered in this cookbook. You will learn how this tool may improve your cooking efficiency and taste.

Here are a few recipes that will highlight all the features of your food processor. This cookbook offers all the recipes you need, whether you want to make a simple sauce, a filling soup, or tasty handmade bread. Designed with newbies in mind, each recipe provides easy-to-follow steps for making the most of your food processor.

Indulge in a world of endless culinary possibilities and elevate your cooking experience with the help of your trusty food processor.

GETTING STARTED WITH YOUR FOOD PROCESSOR

Understanding Your Food Processor: Get to know your food processor's components, such as the bowl, cover, blade attachments, and discs. Gain an understanding of their roles and the value they add to the process of cooking.

Safety First: Advice on how to take care of your food processor properly so that it lasts as long as possible and doesn't cause any mishaps during use.

Basic Operations: Instructions on how to chop, slice, shred, and purée basic foods. In this part, you will learn how to use your machine's various attachments and adjust its settings.

ESSENTIAL TECHNIQUES AND TIPS

Preparation Techniques: Mastering pre-processing steps is essential, so be sure to chop veggies into consistent sizes before you start processing.

Maintenance and Cleaning: Proven methods for keeping your food processor clean and in top operating condition.

Troubleshooting: Things like how to fix blades that seem dull or restore a machine that won't turn on are examples of common problems.

Creative Uses: Creative ways to use your food processor that go beyond the obvious, including making your dough, sauces, and dips.

Recipe Tips: Some ideas for making your go-to recipes work in a food processor, such as modifying the cooking time or adding other ingredients.

BLUEBERRY SMOOTHIE

Total Time: 5 minutes | Prep Time: 5 minutes

Ingredients:

1 cup frozen blueberries	One ripe banana
1 cup unsweetened almond milk	One tablespoon of chia seeds
One tablespoon of honey	½ teaspoon vanilla extract
½ cup Greek yogurt (optional for extra creaminess)	Ice cubes (optional for thicker consistency)

Directions:

(1)Put the frozen blueberries, banana, almond milk, chia seeds, honey (maple syrup or honey), and vanilla essence into a high-speed blender or food processor. Blend or process until smooth. Blend or process until smooth. Blend until it is completely smooth. Before finishing, sprinkle in the chia seeds. (2)Adding Greek yogurt to the mixture will give it a creamier texture. Adding Greek yogurt to the mixture will give it a creamier texture. (3)Using a high speed, blend until the mixture is smooth and creamy. Blend the mixture once more after adding a few ice cubes if you want it to have a more substantial consistency. (4)Assess the sweetness of the dish by tasting it and, if necessary, adding additional honey or maple syrup. (5)After pouring the smoothie into a glass, you should immediately start enjoying it.

CLASSIC GUACAMOLE

Total Time: 10 minutes | Prep Time: 10 minutes

Ingredients:

Three ripe avocados	One small red onion, finely chopped
One medium tomato, diced	1-2 cloves garlic, minced
1 small jalapeño, seeded and finely chopped (optional, for heat)	Juice of 1 lime
¼ cup fresh cilantro, chopped	Salt and pepper to taste

Directions:

1.Once the avocados have been sliced in half, the pit should be removed, and the flesh should be placed in a food processor. (2)Fill the food processor with the chopped red onion, diced tomato, minced garlic, jalapeño (if desired), lime juice, and fresh cilantro. (3)Make sure the guacamole is the consistency you want by pulsing the ingredients until you get the right texture. (4)To taste, season with salt and pepper, depending on your preferences. If you wish to add seasoning, pulse it a few more times like you normally would. (5)Quickly pour the guacamole into a dish and top salads, tacos, burritos, or tortilla chips with it. Serve immediately with veggie sticks or tortilla chips.

CHERRY COMPOTE

Total Time: 20 minutes | Prep Time: 5 minutes

Ingredients

2 cups fresh or frozen cherries, pitted	1/4 cup sugar (adjust based on the sweetness
1 tablespoon lemon juice	1/4 cup water
1 teaspoon vanilla extract	

Directions:

(1)Gather Your Ingredients: Pit the fresh cherries and throw them into the food processor if you're using them. (2)The Cherries Need Processing: In a food processor, pulse the cherries until they are roughly chopped, just a few seconds. (3)Putting the chopped cherries, sugar, lemon juice, and water into a medium-sized saucepan is the first step in making the compote. Bring to a boil over a heat setting medium. (4)It is necessary to bring the liquid to a boil, and after that, the heat should be decreased to a medium-low setting. Maintain a low simmer for ten to fifteen minutes, stirring the mixture often or until the cherries become more malleable, whichever comes first. (5)Take it off the heat and mix in the vanilla essence. (6)Just give it a little time to cool down before you dig in. Refrigerate for up to seven days if stored in an airtight container

ORANGE MACAROONS

Total Time: 40 minutes| Prep Time: 15 minute

Ingredients:

2 cups unsweetened shredded coconut	1/2 cup sugar
Zest of 1 orange	3 large egg whites
1/4 teaspoon salt	1 teaspoon vanilla extract

Directions:

(1)A temperature of 325 degrees Fahrenheit (or 160 degrees Celsius) should be set in the oven before beginning the preparation of the components. Put parchment paper on a baking pan. (2)Do the best you can with what you have: In order to achieve a somewhat chunkier consistency, give the shredded coconut a few pulses in a food processor. Incorporate the sugar and zest from the orange, egg whites, salt, and vanilla essence. Blend or pulse until all ingredients are incorporated and slightly damp. (3)Gather the Ingredients: Drop a heaping spoonful of the mixture onto the baking sheet that has been lined with parchment paper. (4)Put in the Oven and bake for twenty to twenty-five minutes or until the macaroons turn a golden brown color. (5)Before serving, let the macaroons cool entirely on a wire rack. Keep in a sealed container for a maximum of seven days.

SPINACH FRITTERS

Total Time: 30 minutes| Prep Time: 10 minutes

Ingredients:

3 cups fresh spinach leaves,	1/2 cup feta cheese, crumbled
1/4 cup all-purpose flour	2 large eggs
2 green onions, chopped	1/4 cup fresh parsley, chopped
Salt and pepper, to taste	Olive oil for frying

Directions

(1)Get Everything Ready: Grind the spinach to a fine powder in a food processor. (2)To prepare the Batter, place the chopped spinach, feta cheese, flour, eggs, green onions, parsley, salt, and pepper in a mixing bowl. Blend into a smooth mixture. (3)It is necessary to prepare the oil by heating a couple of teaspoons of olive oil in a big skillet until it reaches a temperature that is around medium. (4)To make the fritters, scoop small spoonfuls of the spinach mixture into a skillet and press down with a spatula to flatten. Turn over and cook for another three to four minutes or until golden brown. (5)Remove any extra oil from the fritters by transferring them to a paper towel-lined dish. Once drained, serve. Warm it up and top it with your favorite dipping sauce.

SWEET POTATO FRITTERS

Total Time: 30 minutes| Prep Time: 15 minutes

Ingredients:

2 medium sweet potatoes	1 small onion, roughly chopped
1 clove garlic	1/4 cup fresh parsley or cilantro

1/2 cup all-purpose flour
1 tsp ground cumin
Salt and pepper, to taste
2 large eggs
1/2 tsp smoked paprika
3-4 tbsp olive oil for frying

Directions:

(1)Start by pulsing the sweet potatoes in a food processor until they are finely shredded. Set aside. Place in a clean basin. (2)Get the Batter Mixing: In a food processor, combine the parsley, garlic, and onion. Mince the garlic cloves. Combine them with the sweet potatoes in the basin. (3)Whisk Together: In a bowl, combine the flour, eggs, cumin, smoked paprika, salt, and pepper. Once a batter develops, mix thoroughly to incorporate. 4.Applying olive oil to a large skillet and placing it over a medium heat setting will allow you to make the fritters. Applying olive oil to a large skillet and placing it over a medium heat setting will allow you to make the fritters. Before flattening each fritter in the pan, scoop out two or three teaspoons of the mixture. (5)In a frying pan, cook the mixture for three to four minutes, turning once, or until crackly brown and crispy. Place the pieces on paper towels so that they can drain. (6)Hot serving is best served with extra parsley or sour cream if preferred.

CILANTRO LIME RICE

Total Time: 25 minutes| Prep Time: 5 minutes

Ingredients

1 cup long-grain white rice
1/2 tsp salt
1/2 cup fresh cilantro leaves
1 clove garlic
2 cups water
1 tbsp olive oil
1 lime, juiced and zested
Salt and pepper, to taste

Directions:

(1)Prepare the Cilantro and Lime: In a medium saucepan, combine the rice, water, salt, and olive oil. (2)The rice should be brought to a boil once the water has been absorbed and it has reached the appropriate tenderness. (3)You should immediately reduce the heat to a low setting, cover the pot, and continue to simmer the rice for fifteen to twenty minutes after it has attained the desired level of tenderness. While this is going on, use a food processor to cut the garlic, lime zest, lime juice, and cilantro into very small pieces. (4)Then, combine the cooked rice with the cilantro-lime mixture. Season with salt and pepper to taste. Serve warm as a side dish.

FRUIT COMPOTE

Total Time: 15 minutes| Prep Time: 5 minutes

Cook Time: 10 minutes

Ingredients:

1 cup strawberries, hulled
1 cup raspberries
1 tbsp lemon juice
1/2 tsp ground cinnamon (optional)
1 cup blueberries
1/4 cup honey or maple syrup
1 tsp vanilla extract

Directions:

(1)The fruit should be prepared by pulsing strawberries several times in a food processor until they are finely chopped. Make sure to keep raspberries and blueberries whole. (2)Prepare Compote: Put chopped berries (strawberries, blueberries, raspberries), honey, lemon juice, vanilla essence, and cinnamon (if using) into a medium pot. Keep stirring the mixture occasionally while it is simmering over medium heat for eight to ten minutes or until the fruit is mushy and syrupy, whichever occurs first. (3)Before serving, allow the compote to cool somewhat. Whether it's warm or cold, it goes well with yogurt, ice cream, pancakes, and waffles.

PISTACHIO CHEESE

Total Time: 2 hours | Prep Time: 15 minutes

Ingredients:

1 cup raw pistachios, soaked for 4 hours and drained	1/4 cup nutritional yeast
2 tablespoons lemon juice	2 tablespoons olive oil
1/2 teaspoon garlic powder	1/2 teaspoon onion powder
1/2 teaspoon salt	1/4 teaspoon black pepper
1/4 cup water (as needed)	

Directions:

(1)The fruit should be prepared by pulsing strawberries several times in a food processor until they are finely chopped. Make sure to keep raspberries and blueberries whole. (2)Prepare Compote: Put chopped berries (strawberries, blueberries, raspberries), honey, lemon juice, vanilla essence, and cinnamon (if using) into a medium pot. Keep stirring the mixture occasionally while it is simmering over medium heat for eight to ten minutes or until the fruit is mushy and syrupy, whichever occurs first. (3)Before serving, allow the compote to cool somewhat. Whether it's warm or cold, it goes well with yogurt, ice cream, pancakes, and waffles.

PISTACHIO MILK YOGURT

Total Time: 8 hours | Prep Time: 15 minutes

Ingredients:

1 cup raw pistachios, soaked for 4 hours and drained	2 cups water
1 tablespoon maple syrup or honey (optional)	1 probiotic capsule or 1/4 teaspoon yogurt starter

Directions:

(1)Pistachio Soak: Allow the pistachios to soak in water for approximately four hours. Give them a good rinsing and drain. (2)To make the milk, combine the soaked pistachios with 2 cups of water and pulse in a food processor. Whip till silky smooth. (3)It is recommended that you first pour the mixture into a dish and then make use of a cheesecloth or a nut milk bag to extract as much liquid as possible. This will allow you to strain the milk successfully. (4)Sweeten with Maple Syrup or Honey: (Optional) Whisk the strained milk with the sweetener. (5)Incorporate Probiotic: After opening the probiotic capsule, whisk the powder into the pistachio milk until thoroughly combined. (6)The milk needs to ferment for 6-8 hours at room temperature, so pour it into a clean jar, cover it with a towel, and set it aside. (7)After the yogurt has thickened, put it in the fridge for at least two hours to chill and set. Before serving, mix thoroughly.

GUACAMOLE DIP

Ttal Time: 10 minutes | Prep Time: 10 minutes

Ingredients:

3 ripe avocados	1 small onion, chopped
1 medium tomato, diced	1 jalapeño, seeded and chopped
2 tablespoons lime juice	2 tablespoons cilantro, chopped
1 clove garlic, minced	Salt and pepper to taste

Directions:

(1) Avocado Preparation: In a food processor, puree the avocado flesh after halving the fruit and removing the seeds. Incorporate Elements: The food processor should be stocked with chopped onion, diced tomato, jalapeño, lime juice, cilantro, and minced garlic **(2)**. Blend: Incorporate the guacamole until it achieves the texture you choose, be it thick or smooth. Depending on your personal preferences, you can enhance the flavor of the dish by seasoning it with salt and pepper. **(3)** This will enhance the flavor. When you are ready to serve the mixture, pour it into a bowl and serve it with tortilla chips or vegetable sticks. This will accomplish the task of serving the combination.

GREEK YOGURT DIP

Total Time: 10 minutes | Prep Time: 10 minutes

Ingredients:

- 1 cup Greek yogurt
- 1 tbsp fresh dill, chopped
- 1 tbsp fresh chives, chopped
- Salt and pepper, to taste
- 1 clove garlic, minced
- 1 tbsp fresh parsley, chopped
- 1 tbsp lemon juice

Directions:

(1) A food processor should be used to combine the lemon juice, dill, parsley, chives, garlic, and Greek yogurt. Whisk all of these ingredients together. **(2)** Mix Everything together until it's smooth. **(3)** The amount of salt and pepper to add depends on personal preference. **(4)** After transferring to a serving bowl, let the flavors combine by chilling for at least 10 minutes before serving.

QUESO DIP

Total Time: 15 minutes | Prep Time: 5 minutes

Ingredients:

- 2 cups shredded cheddar cheese
- 1 cup evaporated milk
- 1 jalapeño, seeded and chopped
- 1/2 tsp cumin
- Chopped cilantro for garnish
- 1 cup shredded Monterey Jack cheese
- 1 tbsp cornstarch
- 1 clove garlic, minced
- Salt, to taste

Directions:

(1) Combine the cornstarch and shredded cheese in a food processor. **(2)** Before adding the evaporated milk, jalapeño, garlic, and cumin to the cheese mixture, transfer it to a saucepan. **(3)** While stirring continuously, cook for approximately five to seven minutes over medium heat or until the cheese melts and the mixture thickens. **(4)** Taste and add salt as desired. Top with chopped cilantro and enjoy while still warm.

SMOKED SALMON DIP

Total Time: 15 minutes | Prep Time: 10 minutes

Chill Time: 5 minutes

Ingredients:

- 8 oz smoked salmon
- 1/4 cup sour cream
- 1 tbsp capers, drained
- Salt and pepper, to taste
- 8 oz cream cheese, softened
- 1 tbsp lemon juice
- 1 tbsp fresh dill, chopped

Directions:

(1)Pulse the smoked salmon in a food processor until it's finely chopped. (2)Proceed to incorporate the sour cream, cream cheese, lemon juice, capers, and dill. (3)Whisk or mix until combined. Add more salt and pepper to taste. (4)Put in the fridge for a minimum of five minutes before serving after transferring to a serving platter.

BROCCOLI FRITTERS

Total Time: 30 minutes | Prep Time: 10 minutes

Ingredients:

2 cups broccoli florets	1/2 cup all-purpose flour
1/4 cup grated Parmesan cheese	2 large eggs
2 cloves garlic, minced	1/2 tsp salt
1/4 tsp black pepper	1/4 cup chopped scallions
2 tbsp olive oil, for frying	

Directions:

(1)Toss the broccoli florets in a food processor and pulse until finely chopped. (2)Combine the chopped broccoli with the eggs, flour, Parmesan, garlic, salt, pepper, and scallions in a mixing bowl. Blend into a smooth mixture. (3)A big skillet with olive oil in it should be heated over medium heat. (4)Flatten slightly with a spatula after scooping approximately 2 teaspoons of ingredients for each fritter. (5)Bake for three to four minutes on each side to create a finish that is golden brown and crispy. (6)Transfer the mixture to a plate that has been lined with paper towels in order to soak up any extra grease that may have been there. Before plating, it should be warmed up.

RED VELVET ENERGY BALLS

Total Time: 15 minutes | Prep Time: 15 minutes

Ingredients:

1 cup rolled oats	1/2 cup almond flour
1/4 cup cocoa powder	1/4 cup beetroot powder (for red color)
1/2 cup almond butter	1/4 cup honey or maple syrup
1 tsp vanilla extract	1/4 cup mini dark chocolate chips

Directions:

(1)Run the rolled oats through a food processor until they reach a consistency similar to that of flour. (2)Flour made from almonds, cocoa powder, powder made from beets, almond butter, honey (or maple syrup), and vanilla essence should be added. Flour made from almonds, cocoa powder, powder made from beets, almond butter, honey (or maple syrup), and vanilla essence should be added. Pulse until a dough forms. (3)Fold in the mini chocolate chips. (4)Take a small amount of the contents and roll them into balls. You may keep it in the refrigerator for up to a week if you store it in an airtight container.

S'MORES ENERGY BALLS

Total Time: 15 minutes | Prep Time: 15 minutes

Ingredients:

1 cup rolled oats	1/2 cup graham cracker crumbs
1/2 cup mini marshmallows	1/2 cup chocolate chips
1/2 cup almond butter	1/4 cup honey (or maple syrup)
1/4 cup chopped nuts (optional)	1/2 tsp vanilla extract

Directions:

(1)Mix All Ingredients: Pulverize the crushed graham crackers and rolled oats in a food processor. Blend until combined, then pulse. (2)Honey, almond butter, and vanilla extract are the wet ingredients that must be added. Blend or process until a cohesive mixture forms. (3)Add the Extras: If desired, mix in the chopped nuts, small marshmallows, and chocolate chips. Toss them in until they're well combined. (4)The dough should be rolled into little balls that are roughly one inch in diameter in order to produce balls. Use your hands or a tiny cookie scoop, whatever you choose. (5)It is strongly suggested that the balls be stored in the refrigerator after they have been set on a baking sheet or dish that has been lined with parchment paper. This should be done after the balls have been deposited. Cool the balls in the fridge after transferring them from the oven to a baking sheet or dish lined with parchment paper. The recommended next step is this. This is because the balls will need to be chilled in order to maintain their consistency. Place in the refrigerator for fifty minutes or until it reaches the desired consistency. (6)When stored in the refrigerator, energy balls can be kept for up to seven days if they are adequately sealed.

CASHEW MILK SMOOTHIE

Total Time: 5 minutes | Prep Time: 5 minutes

Ingredients:

1 cup cashew milk (store-bought or homemade)	1 banana (preferably frozen)
1/2 cup spinach or kale	1 tbsp honey or maple syrup
1/2 tsp vanilla extract	1/2 cup ice cubes

Directions:

(1)Combine Combining the cashew milk, banana, spinach or kale (if used), honey or maple syrup, vanilla essence, and ice cubes in a blender is the first step in making this smoothie. (2)Process: Blend until smooth and creamy. In case the smoothie turns out too thick, just add a splash or two extra cashew milk to get the right consistency. In case the smoothie turns out too thick, just add a splash or two extra cashew milk to get the right consistency. (3)Pour the mixture into a glass, and then get ready to drink it right away.

GINGERBREAD COOKIES

Total Time: 1 hour | Prep Time: 20 minutes

Ingredients:

2 ¾ cups all-purpose flour	1 teaspoon baking soda
2 teaspoons ground ginger	1 ½ teaspoons ground cinnamon
¼ teaspoon ground cloves	¼ teaspoon salt
½ cup unsalted butter, softened	⅓ cup brown sugar, packed
1 large egg	¼ cup molasses

Directions:

(1)Concoct For this recipe, you will need to use a blender to combine the following Ingredients: cashew milk, banana, spinach, or kale (if you are using it), honey or maple syrup, vanilla essence, and ice cubes. Concoct For this recipe, you will need to use a blender to combine the following Ingredients: cashew milk, banana, spinach, or kale (if you are using it), honey or maple syrup, vanilla essence, and ice cubes. (2)Concoct For this recipe, you will need to use a blender to combine the following Ingredients: cashew milk, banana, spinach, or kale (if you are using it), honey or maple syrup, vanilla essence, and ice cubes. (3)Fill a glass with the mixture and savor it right away to serve.

VANILLA ENERGY BALLS

Total Time: 20 minutes | Prep Time: 10 minutes

Ingredients:

1 cup rolled oats	½ cup almond butter
¼ cup honey or maple syrup	¼ cup shredded coconut
1 tablespoon vanilla extract	¼ cup mini chocolate chips (optional)

Directions:

(1) Chop the almond butter, oats, honey, coconut, and vanilla essence into a food processor. Mix until Everything is mixed and the mixture becomes sticky. (2) Chocolate chips can be folded in if desired. (3) Shape the dough into balls no larger than an inch and set them on a baking pan. (4) Set in the fridge for 10 minutes, minimum.

CREAMY AVOCADO DIP

Total Time: 10 minutes | Prep Time: 10 minutes

Ingredients:

2 ripe avocados	1 lime, juiced
1 clove garlic	¼ cup chopped fresh cilantro
½ teaspoon salt	¼ teaspoon ground cumin

Directions:

(1) Toss the avocados with the lime juice, garlic, cilantro, salt, and cumin in a food processor. (2) Whisk or mix until combined. Salt and pepper to taste. (3) You can serve it immediately after garnishing it with chips or veggies, or you can store it in the refrigerator in an airtight container for later use.

PUMPKIN SEED ENERGY BALLS

Total Time: 20 minutes | Prep Time: 10 minutes

Ingredients:

1 cup raw pumpkin seeds	½ cup pitted dates
¼ cup almond butter	¼ cup honey
½ teaspoon ground cinnamon	

Directions:

(1) Crush the pumpkin seeds to a powder in a food processor. (2) Honey, cinnamon, almond butter, and dates should be added. After the ingredients have combined, process until a sticky dough forms. (3) Shape the dough into balls no larger than an inch and set them on a baking pan. (4) Set aside to harden up in the fridge for at least 10 minutes.

RASPBERRY ENERGY BALLS

Total Time: 20 minutes

| Prep Time: 10 minutes

Ingredients:

1 cup dried raspberries	1 cup rolled oats
½ cup almond flour	¼ cup almond butter
2 tablespoons honey	

Directions:

(1) Grind the dried raspberries to a fine powder in a food processor. (2) Honey, almond butter, almond flour, and oats should be added. Stir until all ingredients are mixed and the mixture becomes sticky. (3) On a baking sheet, roll the dough into 1-inch balls. (4) Set in the fridge for 10 minutes, minimum.

FLAXSEED CHEESE

Total Time: 1 hour | Prep Time: 10 minutes

Ingredients:

1 cup raw cashews,	½ cup flaxseeds
¼ cup nutritional yeast	1 tablespoon lemon juice
1 garlic clove	½ teaspoon salt

Directions:

(1) After the cashews have been soaked, drain and rinse them well. Toss the cashews, flaxseeds, nutritional yeast, garlic, lemon juice, and salt in a food processor. **(2)** Whisk or mix until combined. Salt and pepper to taste. **(3)** Put it in the fridge for 30 minutes to set, then transfer it to a container.

PROTEIN ENERGY BALLS

Total Time: 20 minutes | Prep Time: 10 minutes

Ingredients:

1 cup rolled oats	1/2 cup nut butter
1/2 cup honey or maple syrup	1/4 cup chia seeds
1/4 cup protein powder (optional)	1/4 cup mini chocolate chips
1/2 tsp vanilla extract	

Directions:

(1) Set the food processor at high speed and add all ingredients. **(2)** Mix Everything together until it begins to clump together, then pulse. **(3)** Form the mixture into balls no larger than a 1 inch ball. **(4)** On a parchment-lined baking sheet, arrange the balls. **(5)** Put in the fridge for half an hour or until it sets.

SPICY GARLIC HERB RUB

Total Time: 10 minutes | Prep Time: 10 minutes

Ingredients:

1 cup unsalted butter, softened	4 cloves garlic, minced
1 tbsp fresh parsley, chopped	1 tbsp fresh chives, chopped
1/2 tsp dried oregano	1/4 tsp salt
1/4 tsp black pepper	

Directions:

(1) Go ahead and put Everything in the food processor. **(2)** Mix until blended and completely smooth. **(3)** Move to a storage container and keep in the fridge until needed.

CRAB RANGOON DIP

Total Time: 30 minutes | Prep Time: 10 minutes

Ingredients:

1 cup cooked crab meat	1 cup cream cheese, softened
1/2 cup sour cream	1/4 cup mayonnaise
1/4 cup green onions, chopped	1 tsp garlic powder
1 tsp Worcestershire sauce	Salt and pepper to taste

Directions:

(1) Place all of the ingredients into the food processor and process until they are completely smooth. **(2)** Whisk or mix until combined. **(3)** Place in the Oven and cook for 20 minutes, or until heated through and bubbling, at 375°F **(4)** (190°C). **(5)** Pair with crackers, tortilla chips, or bread.

BEET FRITTERS

Total Time: 30 minutes | Prep Time: 15 minutes

Ingredients:

2 medium beets,	1/2 cup grated onion

peeled and grated
1/2 cup all-purpose flour
1 egg, beaten
Salt and pepper to taste
1/4 cup cornmeal
1/2 tsp baking powder
Olive oil for frying

Directions:

(1) Grate the beets and onion and pulse them in a food processor until they are finely minced. (2) Incorporate the cornmeal, flour, baking powder, salt, and pepper into the mixture after transferring it to a bowl. (3) The olive oil should be warmed up in a skillet that is set over medium heat. (4) Spoon the mixture into the skillet in spoonfuls and press down with a spatula to flatten. (5) Cook, flipping once, for three to four minutes or until crisp and golden. (6) Before serving, drain well using paper towels.

HUMMUS DIP

Total Time: 10 minutes | Prep Time: 10 minutes

Ingredients:

1 can (15 oz) chickpeas
1/4 cup tahini
2 tablespoons extra-virgin olive oil
Salt to taste
1/4 cup fresh lemon juice
1 small garlic clove, minced
1/2 teaspoon ground cumin
2 to 3 tablespoons water, as needed

Directions:

Toss the chickpeas with the garlic, tahini, lemon juice, cumin, olive oil, and food processor. Whip till completely smooth. (2) Add water, tablespoon by tablespoon, until the mixture reaches the consistency you desire if it's too thick. (3) After processing, add salt according to your taste. (4) Serve with pita bread and vegetables, or use as a spread after transferring to a bowl and drizzling with a little olive oil.

BLUE CHEESE DIP

Total Time: 10 minutes | Prep Time: 10 minutes

Ingredients:

1 cup sour cream
1/2 cup crumbled blue cheese
1 tablespoon chopped fresh chives (optional)
1/2 cup mayonnaise
1 tablespoon lemon juice
Salt and black pepper to taste

Directions:

(1) Throw the blue cheese, sour cream, and mayonnaise into a food processor. Incorporate the blue cheese chunks into the mixture while processing until it becomes smooth. (2) Finish with salt, pepper, lemon juice, and chives, if desired. To combine, pulse several times. (3) Review the seasoning and make any required adjustments. (4) Put in the fridge for 30 minutes to let the flavors combine after transferring to a serving bowl, as a dip, on wings, or with vegetables.

NUTELLA

Total Time: 10 minutes | Prep Time: 10 minutes

Ingredients:

1 cup hazelnuts, toasted
1/4 cup unsweetened cocoa powder
1/4 cup vegetable oil
A pinch of salt
1 cup powdered sugar
1/4 cup milk
1 teaspoon vanilla extract

Directions:

(1)Throw the blue cheese, sour cream, and mayonnaise into a food processor. Incorporate the blue cheese chunks into the mixture while processing until it becomes smooth. (2)Finish with salt, pepper, lemon juice, and chives, if desired. To combine, pulse several times. (3)Review the seasoning and make any required adjustments. (4)Put in the fridge for 30 minutes to let the flavors combine after transferring to a serving bowl, as a dip, on wings, or with vegetables.

QUINOA ENERGY BALLS

Total Time: 15 minutes | Prep Time: 15 minutes

Ingredients:

- 1 cup cooked quinoa (cooled)
- 1/2 cup almond butter
- 1/4 cup mini chocolate chips
- 1/2 cup rolled oats
- 1/4 cup honey
- 1/4 cup chia seeds

Directions:

(1)Cook the quinoa and oats, and then add the almond butter, honey, and chia seeds. Pulse until well combined. Mix Everything together by pulsing. (2)You have the option of including chocolate chips or dried fruit in the mixture, and after that, you can give it a quick pulse to ensure that everything is thoroughly combined. (3)After rolling after rolling the dough into little balls, set them on a parchment-lined baking sheet. Little balls set them on a parchment-lined baking sheet. Bake for about 20 minutes. Bake for around half an hour. (4)Put in the fridge for half an hour or until it sets. Keep in the fridge for up to a week if sealed tightly.

PEANUT BUTTER ENERGY BALLS

Total Time: 15 minutes | Prep Time: 15 minutes

Ingredients:

- 1 cup rolled oats
- 1/4 cup honey or maple syrup
- 1/4 cup mini chocolate chips (optional
- 1/2 cup peanut butter
- 1/4 cup ground flaxseed

Directions:

(1)Blend together the peanut butter, oats, honey, and flaxseed in a food processor. Blend or process until a cohesive mixture forms. (2)Pulse a few times to combine, then add chocolate chips if using. (3)The dough should be rolled into little balls and placed on a baking pan coated with parchment paper. (4)Put in the fridge for half an hour or until it sets. Keep in the fridge for up to a week if sealed tightly.

PUMPKIN SPICE COMPOTE

Total Time: 25 minutes | Prep Time: 10 minutes

Ingredients:

- 2 cups canned pumpkin
- 1/4 cup maple syrup
- 1/2 teaspoon ground cinnamon
- 1/4 teaspoon ground ginger
- 1/2 cup brown sugar
- 1 teaspoon pumpkin pie spice
- 1/4 teaspoon ground nutmeg
- 1/4 cup water

Directions:

(1)The canned pumpkin should be added to the food processor along with the pumpkin puree, brown sugar, maple syrup, cinnamon, ginger, nutmeg, and pumpkin pie spice. Other ingredients include maple syrup. (2)Combine ingredients and mix until creamy. (3)Add the water while stirring the mixture in a saucepan. (4)After approximately fifteen minutes of cooking over medium heat, the compote should have thickened and reached the desired temperature. During this time, you should stir it frequently during the cooking process. (5)Chill before you eat. Keep in the fridge for up to two weeks if sealed tightly.

CHIPOTLE DIP

Total Time: 10 minutes | Prep Time: 10 minutes

Ingredients:

- 1 cup sour cream
- 1-2 chipotle peppers in adobo sauce (adjust based on desired spice level)
- 1 tablespoon lime juice
- Salt to taste
- 1/2 cup mayonnaise
- 1 clove garlic
- 1/2 teaspoon ground cumin

Directions:

(1)Step into the food processor and add the chipotle peppers, sour cream, mayonnaise, garlic, lime juice, and cumin. (2)Mix until blended and completely smooth. (3)Taste and add salt as desired. (4)Put it in the fridge for half an hour before you serve it so the flavors can (5)Meld.

SMOOTHIE BASE

Total Time: 5 minutes | Prep Time: 5 minutes

Ingredients:

- 1 cup Greek yogurt
- 1 banana
- 1 tablespoon honey
- 1/2 cup orange juice
- 1/2 cup frozen berries

Directions:

(1)Blend together the Greek yogurt, orange juice, banana, frozen berries, and honey (if desired) in a food processor. (2)Whisk or mix until combined. (3)Refrigerate for up to two days before use or use right away.

CRANBERRY COMPOTE

Total Time: 20 minutes | Prep Time: 10 minutes

Ingredients:

- 2 cups fresh or frozen cranberries
- 1/2 cup water
- 1/4 teaspoon ground cinnamon
- 1 cup sugar
- 1/2 teaspoon grated orange zest
- 1/4 teaspoon ground allspice

Directions:

(1)Add sugar and cranberries to a pot that has been filled with water until it is halfway full. (2)Stir often while you bring it to a boil in a medium saucepan. (3)Turn the heat down to low and continue to boil the mixture for around ten to fifteen minutes after the cranberries have popped and the sauce has reached a more cohesive consistency. (4)Add orange zest, cinnamon, and allspice and mix well. (5)Wait till it reaches room temperature before you eat it. Keep in the fridge for up to two weeks if sealed tightly.

HONEY BUTTER

Total Time: 5 minutes | Prep Time: 5 minutes

Ingredients:

- 1/2 cup unsalted butter, softened
- 1/2 teaspoon ground cinnamon (optional
- 1/4 cup honey

Directions:

(1) Butter that has been softened, honey, and ground cinnamon (if you are using it) should be placed in the food processor. (2) Mix until it is completely smooth and properly blended. (3) Place in a bowl or jar, then place in the refrigerator until it becomes hard. At room temperature, serve the dish.

OATMEAL ENERGY BALLS

Total Time: 15 minutes | Prep Time: 15 minutes

Ingredients:

- 1 cup rolled oats
- 1/4 cup honey
- 1/4 cup chia seeds or flaxseeds (optional)
- 1/2 cup nut butter
- 1/4 cup mini chocolate chips
- 1/2 teaspoon vanilla extract

Directions:

(1) Mince the nuts, add the honey (or maple syrup), and pulse until combined. Add the rolled oats and nut butter. (2) The mixture will begin to come together as you blend. Chocolate chips, dried fruit, chia seeds, or flaxseeds can be added if desired. (3) Form little balls with scooped-out tablespoons. (4) After 30 minutes of chilling in the fridge, the energy balls should be solid enough to serve.

QUINOA BURGERS

Total Time: 45 minutes | Prep Time: 15 minutes

Ingredients:

- 1 cup cooked quinoa
- 1/2 cup finely chopped onion
- One can (15 oz) black beans
- 1/2 cup finely chopped bell pepper
- 1/2 cup grated carrot
- 2 cloves garlic, minced
- 1/4 teaspoon paprika
- 1/4 teaspoon black pepper
- 1/4 cup breadcrumbs
- 1/4 cup fresh parsley
- 1/2 teaspoon cumin
- 1/4 teaspoon salt
- 1 egg

Directions:

(1) Put the black beans in a food processor and puree them until they are almost completely broken up. (2) Include the quinoa, carrot, onion, pepper, parsley, garlic, cumin, paprika, salt, and pepper. Mix by pulsing. (3) After transferring to a bowl, mix in the breadcrumbs and egg. (4) Form patties with the mixture. (5) To make the patties golden brown and heated through, heat a skillet over medium heat and cook for 7 to 10 minutes per side.

GINGER PEAR COMPOTE

Total Time: 25 minutes | Prep Time: 10 minutes

Ingredients:

- 4 ripe pears, peeled, cored, and chopped
- 1/4 cup honey or maple syrup
- 1/2 teaspoon ground cinnamon
- 1 tablespoon grated fresh ginger
- 1/4 cup water
- 1/4 teaspoon ground nutmeg

Directions:

(1) The diced pears, ginger, honey (or maple syrup), water, cinnamon, and nutmeg should be mixed together in a pot of around medium size. (2) It should be brought to a boil over medium heat, and then it should be reduced to a simmer. (3) The pears should be cooked for fifteen to twenty minutes, with stirring occurring occasionally, until they are soft and the liquid has thickened. (4) Let the compote cool before serving, or store it in the refrigerator for up to a week.

GREEN SMOOTHIE

Total Time: 5 minutes | Prep Time: 5 minutes

Ingredients:

1 cup fresh spinach or kale	1 banana
1/2 cup frozen pineapple chunks	1/2 cup frozen mango chunks
1 cup almond milk	1 tablespoon chia seeds (optional)
1 teaspoon honey or maple syrup (optional)	

Directions:

(1)All of the ingredients should be mixed together in a blender or food processor. (2)Blend until it is completely smooth. (3)Evaluate the sweetness of the dish and, if necessary, correct it by adding honey or maple syrup. (4)You should immediately pour it into a glass and drink it.

NUT BUTTER ENERGY BALLS

Total Time: 15 minutes | Prep Time: 15 minutes

Ingredients:

1 cup oats	1/2 cup nut butter
1/4 cup honey	1/4 cup ground flaxseed
1/4 cup mini chocolate chips	1/2 teaspoon vanilla extract

Directions:

A food processor should be used to combine the oats, nut butter, honey (or maple syrup), and vanilla extract. Next, the mixture should be processed. After that, move on to the subsequent stage. (2)All of the components should be mixed together until they start to resemble one another. In the event that you are working with it, you should incorporate chocolate chips or dried fruit in addition to ground flaxseed or chia seeds. (3)To make the balls, scoop out portions that are around the size of a tablespoon and roll them through your hands. (4)Put the energy balls on a plate or baking sheet, and then place them in the refrigerator for at least half an hour so that they can harden.

CHERRY SMOOTHIE

Total Time: 5 minutes | Prep Time: 5 minutes

Ingredients:

1 cup frozen cherries	1 banana
1 cup almond milk	1 tablespoon chia seeds
1 teaspoon maple syrup (optional)	1/2 teaspoon vanilla extract (optional)

Directions:

(1)Blend or process all of the ingredients in a food processor. (2)Whip on high speed until combined. (3)Add additional maple syrup or almond milk to taste and alter sweetness or thickness. (4)Fill a glass with it and savor it right away.

MACADAMIA NUT CHEESE

Total Time: 10 minutes | Prep Time: 10 minutes

Ingredients:

1 cup raw macadamia nuts (soaked for 2-4 hours)	1/4 cup nutritional yeast
1/4 cup water	2 tablespoons lemon juice
1 clove garlic	1/2 teaspoon salt
1/4 teaspoon turmeric (for color, optional)	

Directions:

(1) After the macadamia nuts have soaked, drain and rinse them. Put all of the ingredients into a food processor and mix them together. To ensure that the mixture is totally smooth, scrape down the edges of the blender and continue blending until it is perfectly smooth. Depending on your preference, season with salt and pepper. In the event that the mixture is excessively thick, add a little bit more water. Serve as a dip or spread.

VEGAN GOAT CHEESE

Total Time: 15 minutes | Prep Time: 15 minutes

Ingredients:

- 1 cup raw cashews
- 2 tablespoons nutritional yeast
- 2 tablespoons lemon juice
- 1/4 cup water
- 1 clove garlic
- 1 teaspoon dried thyme
- 1/2 teaspoon salt

Directions:

(1) After soaking the cashews, drain and rinse them. (2) Combine everything in a food processor and blend until smooth. (3) Whip until the mixture is velvety smooth. (4) Review the seasoning and make any required adjustments. (5) Set aside to firm up in the fridge for at least an hour prior to serving.

BROWNIE ENERGY BALLS

Total Time: 15 minutes | Prep Time: 15 minutes

Ingredients:

- 1 cup pitted dates
- 1 cup raw walnuts
- 1/2 cup raw cocoa powder
- 1/4 cup almond butter
- 1/4 cup water
- 1/2 teaspoon vanilla extract (optional)
- Pinch of salt

Directions:

(1) Grind the walnuts and dates together in a food processor until they are finely chopped. (2) Incorporate almond butter, cocoa powder, and a dash of salt. Mix Everything together. (3) When pressing, the mixture should stick together, so add water gradually. (4) Form tiny balls from the mixture. You may keep it in the fridge for up to two weeks..

CASHEW CHOCOLATE SPREAD

Total Time: 10 minutes

| Prep Time: 10 minutes

Ingredients:

- 1 cup raw cashews
- 1/4 cup cocoa powder
- 1/4 cup maple syrup
- 1/4 cup almond milk
- 1/4 teaspoon vanilla extract
- Pinch of salt

Directions:

(1) After soaking the cashews, drain and rinse them. (2) Put everything into a food processor and puree it until smooth. Put everything into a food processor and puree it until smooth. (3) Whisk or mix until combined. (4) If the cocoa powder or sugar is too sweet, taste and add more or less. (5) For a maximum of two weeks, keep in an airtight container in the fridge.

WHITE CHOCOLATE MACADAMIA COOKIES

Total Time: 30 minutes | Prep Time: 15 minutes

Ingredients:

1 cup (2 sticks) unsalted butter, softened	1 cup granulated sugar
1 cup packed brown sugar	2 large eggs
1 tsp vanilla extract	3 cups all-purpose flour
1 tsp baking soda	1/2 tsp salt
1 cup white chocolate chips	1 cup chopped macadamia nuts

Directions:

(1)For best results, combine the brown sugar, granulated sugar, and butter in a food processor before preheating the oven to 350 degrees Fahrenheit. Whip until the mixture is airy and frothy. (2)Put the eggs and vanilla essence in the bowl. Blend Everything together. (3)An additional basin is required for the mixing of flour, baking soda, and salt. (4)Toss the dry ingredients into the food processor one cup at a time and pulse until just mixed. (5)With a spatula, combine the macadamia nuts and white chocolate chips. (6)Spoon dough by the spoonful onto a parchment-lined baking sheet. (7)To get golden brown edges, bake for 10 to 12 minutes. (8)After the pan has cooled slightly, remove the cookies and set them on a wire rack to cool entirely.

SNICKERDOODLE COOKIES

Total Time: 30 minutes | Prep Time: 15 minutes

Ingredients:

1 cup (2 sticks) unsalted butter, softened	1 1/2 cups granulated sugar
2 large eggs	2 3/4 cups all-purpose flour
1/4 tsp baking soda	1/2 tsp baking powder
1/4 tsp salt	1/4 cup granulated sugar (for rolling)
1 tbsp ground cinnamon (for rolling)	

Directions:

(1)Before beginning the baking process, adjust the temperature of the oven to 350 degrees Fahrenheit. (2)The sugar and melted butter can be easily combined using a food processor, which is the ideal instrument for this task. Mince till smooth and velvety. (3)Add the eggs after processing until well combined. (4)Mix the flour, baking soda, baking powder, and salt in a different bowl if you like. Use a whisk to mix the ingredients. (5)When the wet ingredients are almost combined, put them in the food processor and process until a dough forms. (6)Cinnamon and sugar are combined in a small bowl, and once the sugar has been measured, it is poured into a quarter cup. (7)Before rolling in the cinnamon-sugar mixture, roll the dough into 1-inch balls. (8)On a parchment-lined baking sheet, set the coated dough balls. (9)After 10 to 12 minutes in the Oven, you should see some cracking on top and set edges. (10)Moving the cookies from the baking sheet to a wire rack to cool for a little while is the last step before serving.

LATKES

Total Time: 45 minutes | Prep Time: 20 minutes

Ingredients:

4 large russet potatoes, peeled	1 large onion, peeled
2 large eggs	1/4 cup all-purpose flour
1 tsp salt	1/2 tsp black pepper
Vegetable oil for frying	

Directions:

(1)Put the onion and potatoes in a big basin after grating them. (2)Place shredded ingredients on a dry kitchen towel and press to squeeze off excess moisture. Return the drained mixture to the bowl. Add the eggs, flour, salt, and pepper. Mix until everything is well combined in a large pan set over medium heat, and warm approximately 1/4 inch of vegetable oil. (3)\ Spoon the potato mixture into the heated oil and gently press each spoonful down with the back of the spoon to make it flatten. After approximately three or four minutes in the fryer per side, the latkes should be golden brown and crunchy. After transferring the latkes to a paper towel-lined dish, set them aside to soak up any extra oil. After transferring the latkes to a paper towel-lined dish, set them aside to soak up any extra oil.

VEGAN MASCARPONE

Total Time: 10 minutes | Prep Time: 10 minutes

Ingredients:

1 cup raw cashews
1/4 cup lemon juice
1/4 tsp salt
1/4 cup coconut cream
1 tsp vanilla extract

Directions:

(1)After being soaked, cashews should be washed and rinsed before being put into a food processor, along with coconut cream, salt, lemon juice, and vanilla essence. (2)The coconut cream should be the last ingredient. The mixture should be processed until it is completely smooth and velvety. Pour the mascarpone into a container and chill it for at least an hour before serving.

MINESTRONE

Total Time: 1 hour | Prep Time: 15 minutes

Ingredients:

2 tbsp olive oil
1 large onion, chopped
3 cloves garlic, minced
2 celery stalks, diced
1 cup green beans, chopped
1 can (15 oz) diced tomatoes
1 cup pasta (small shapes like elbow or shell)
1 cup fresh spinach or kale
1 tsp dried basil
2 carrots, diced
1 zucchini, diced
1 cup potatoes, diced
4 cups vegetable broth
One can (15 oz) cannellini beans
1 tsp dried oregano
Salt and pepper to taste

Directions:

(1)Put the peaches in the food processor after slicing them into small pieces. (2)Process until a coarse texture is achieved. (3)Move the peach mixture to a medium-sized pot and stir. (4)Combine the sugar, lemon juice, cinnamon, and vanilla extract. (5)Stirring often, cook for approximately 10 to 15 minutes over medium heat or until the peaches collapse and the mixture thickens. (6)Let cool completely before enjoying.

PEACH COMPOTE

Total Time: 20 minutes

| Prep Time: 10 minutes

Ingredients:

4 ripe peaches, peeled and pitted
1 tbsp lemon juice
1/4 tsp ground cinnamon
1/4 cup sugar (or to taste)
1/2 tsp vanilla extract

Directions:

(1)Put the peaches in the food processor after slicing them into small pieces. (2)Process until a coarse texture is achieved. (3)Move the peach mixture to a medium-sized pot and stir.

(4)Combine the sugar, lemon juice, cinnamon, and vanilla extract. (5)Stirring often, cook for approximately 10 to 15 minutes over medium heat or until the peaches collapse and the mixture thickens. (6)Let cool completely before enjoying.

ALMOND BUTTER YOGURT

Total Time: 10 minutes | Prep Time: 10 minutes

Ingredients:

1 cup plain Greek yogurt
1 tbsp honey
Pinch of salt
1/4 cup almond butter
1/2 tsp vanilla extract

Directions:

(1)All of the ingredients should be combined in the food processor. (2)Produce a puree that is silky, smooth, and creamy in texture. (3)It can be served right away, or it can be stored in the refrigerator until it is required.

COCONUT MACAROONS

Total Time: 25 minutes | Prep Time: 10 minutes

Ingredients:

2 cups shredded coconut
1/2 tsp vanilla extract
1/2 cup sweetened condensed milk
Pinch of salt

Directions:

(1)Gather your ingredients and get the oven preheated to 325 degrees Fahrenheit (163 degrees Celsius). Line a baking sheet with parchment paper. Set aside. (2)Combine all ingredients in the food processor. (3)Pulse until the mixture is well combined. (4)Scoop small mounds onto the prepared baking sheet. (5)Bake for 15-20 minutes, or until golden brown. (6)Cool on a wire rack.

GINGERBREAD MACAROONS

Total Time: 30 minutes | Prep Time: 10 minutes

Ingredients:

2 cups shredded coconut
1/2 cup almond flour
1 tsp ground cinnamon
Pinch of salt
1/2 cup molasses
1 tsp ground ginger
1/4 tsp ground cloves

Directions:

(1)Position a baking sheet on top of a parchment-lined baking pan and preheat the oven to 325 degrees Fahrenheit (163 degrees Celsius). (2)Put everything into the food processor and blend until smooth. (3)Blend until combined. (4)Arrange mounds on the baking sheet that has been prepared. (5)To get golden, crisp edges, bake for 15 to 20 minutes. (6)Let cool completely before enjoying.

CHEESY SPINACH DIP

Total Time: 15 minutes | Prep Time: 10 minutes

Ingredients:\

1 cup fresh spinach
1/2 cup grated Parmesan cheese
1/4 cup sour cream
Salt and pepper to taste
1 cup cream cheese, softened
1/2 cup shredded mozzarella cheese
1 garlic clove, minced

Directions:

(1)Combine all ingredients in the food processor. (2)Blend until smooth and creamy. (3)Transfer to a bowl and serve with crackers or bread.

SPICY SALSA

Total Time: 10 minutes | Prep Time: 10 minutes

Ingredients:

4 ripe tomatoes, quartered	1/2 onion, chopped
1 jalapeño, seeded (for less heat) and chopped	2 cloves garlic
1/4 cup fresh cilantro	1 tbsp lime juice
Salt to taste	

Directions:

(1)You may serve this mixture with tortilla chips or as a topping for your favorite foods. Put everything in the food processor and pulse until it reaches the texture you desire, whether that's chunky or smooth. If necessary, adjust the seasoning with salt.

MANGO SMOOTHIE

Total Time: 5 minutes

| Prep Time: 5 minutes

Ingredients:

1 ripe mango, peeled and pitted	1 banana
1/2 cup plain yogurt	1/2 cup orange juice
1 tbsp honey (optional)	

Directions:

(1)All of the ingredients should be combined in the food processor. (2)Blend until it is completely smooth. (3)Spoon the concoction into individual glasses and promptly serve.

FLAXSEED ENERGY BALLS

Total Time: 15 minutes | Prep Time: 10 minutes

Ingredients:

1 cup dates, pitted	1/2 cup flaxseeds
1/2 cup almonds	2 tbsp cocoa powder
1/4 cup shredded coconut	

Directions:

(1)The food processor should be filled with all of the ingredients. (2)Mix until the ingredients are incorporated into one another. (3)Form the mixture into tiny balls. (4)At least half an hour before serving, place the dish in the refrigerator to chill..

AGAVE YOGURT

Total Time: 10 minutes | Prep Time: 10 minutes

Ingredients:

1 cup plain Greek yogurt	2 tbsp agave syrup
1/2 tsp vanilla extract	

Directions:

(1)All of the ingredients should be combined in the food processor. (2)Blend until everything is completely smooth and well combined. (3)Serve immediately, or store in the refrigerator until you are needed.

MAPLE ENERGY BALLS

Total Time: 15 minutes | Prep Time: 10 minutes

Ingredients:

1 cup oats	1/2 cup almond butter
1/4 cup pure maple syrup	1/4 cup chopped nuts (optional)

Directions:

(1)All of the components should be placed in the food processor. (2)Stir the ingredients together until they come together. (3)Create little balls by rolling. (4)Before serving, allow the dish to chill in the refrigerator for at least half an hour.

OATMEAL RAISIN COOKIES

Total Time: 45 minutes | Prep Time: 15 minutes

Ingredients:

1 cup butter, softened	1 cup brown sugar
1/2 cup granulated sugar	2 large eggs
1 tsp vanilla extract	1 1/2 cups all-purpose flour
1/2 tsp baking soda	1/2 tsp baking powder
1/2 tsp salt	3 cups rolled oats
1 cup raisins	

Directions:

(1)Turn the oven on high heat (350°F, 175°C). Roll out parchment paper to line baking sheets. (2)The brown sugar, granulated sugar, and butter should be combined in a food processor until the mixture is light and puffy. (3)Gradually add the eggs while whisking constantly. Add the vanilla extract and stir. (4)A basin containing flour, baking soda, powder, and salt should be mixed thoroughly. Incorporate the ingredients by slowly pouring them into the food processor and mixing just until combined. (5)Add the raisins and oats and mix well. (6)Spoon dough onto the baking sheets that have been preheated. (7)Cook for 12–15 minutes or until the edges start to turn golden. Once the sheets have cooled for a while, transfer them to a wire rack to let them cool completely.

PINEAPPLE SMOOTHIE

Total Time: 10 minutes | Prep Time: 10 minutes

Ingredients:

1 cup pineapple chunks (fresh or frozen)	1 banana
1 cup coconut milk	1 tbsp honey or agave syrup (optional)
1/2 cup ice	

Directions:

(1)All of the ingredients should be placed in a blender or food processor. (2)Blend until it is completely smooth. (3)Transfer the mixture to serving glasses and enjoy it immediately.

VEGAN MOZZARELLA

Total Time: 20 minutes | Prep Time: 10 minutes

Ingredients:

1/2 cup raw cashews	1/2 cup water
1/4 cup nutritional yeast	1 tbsp lemon juice
1 tbsp tapioca starch	1/2 tsp garlic powder
1/2 tsp salt	

Directions:

(1)After soaking the cashews, drain and rinse them. (2)Blend together cashews, water, nutritional yeast, zest of lemon, tapioca starch, garlic powder, salt, and nutritional yeast in a food processor. (3)Mix until completely smooth. (4)To thicken and make it stretchy, transfer the mixture to a saucepan and simmer, stirring continuously, over medium heat. (5)Before using, allow to cool somewhat. Place in a refrigerator-safe container and seal tightly.

MINT MACAROONS

Total Time: 30 minutes | Prep Time: 15 minutes

Ingredients:

2 cups shredded coconut
1/2 tsp peppermint extract
1/2 cup sweetened condensed milk
1/4 cup mini chocolate chips (optional)

Directions:

(1)Get your oven preheated to 325°F (163°C). Put parchment paper on a baking pan. (2)Shredded coconut, sweetened condensed milk, and peppermint extract should be mixed together in a food processor. Thoroughly combine by blending. (3)If using, stir in the chocolate chips. (4)Spoon the batter onto the preheated baking sheet. (5)Cook in the oven for around fifteen to twenty minutes or until a golden flavor develops. (6)After a few minutes of cooling on the baking sheet, move to a wire rack to finish cooling.

GREEN GODDESS DIP

Total Time: 10 minutes | Prep Time: 10 minutes

Ingredients:

1 cup fresh parsley
1/2 cup fresh chives
2 tbsp lemon juice
Salt and pepper to taste
1/2 cup fresh basil
1/2 cup plain Greek yogurt
1 garlic clove

Directions:

(1)Choke or pulse the garlic, parsley, basil, Greek yogurt, lemon juice, and chives until well combined. (2)Combine ingredients and mix until creamy. (3)Taste and add salt and pepper as needed. (4)Dip chips in it or serve with vegetables.

CLASSIC HUMMUS

Total Time: 15 minutes | Prep Time: 10 minutes

Ingredients:

1 can (15 oz) chickpeas
1 garlic clove
1/2 tsp ground cumin
1/4 cup lemon juice
2 tbsp olive oil
Salt to taste

Directions:

(1)Blend together the garlic, lemon juice, tahini, and chickpeas in a food processor. (2)Just add a little water and mix until smooth to get the consistency you need. (3)While the processor is operating, slowly drizzle in the olive oil. (4)As a finishing touch, add salt and ground cumin. Mix it up once again. (5)Add pita bread or fresh vegetables for a side dish.

SPLIT PEA SOUP

Total Time: 1 hour | Prep Time: 15 minutes

Ingredients:

1 cup split peas
2 carrots, chopped
3 garlic cloves, minced
1 bay leaf
Salt and pepper to taste
1 onion, chopped
2 celery stalks, chopped
4 cups vegetable broth
1/2 tsp thyme

Directions:

(1)Blanch the peas by rinsing them in cool water. (2)Chop the garlic, carrots, onion, and celery finely in a food processor. (3)Saute the chopped veggies in a big saucepan until they're tender. (4)Proceed by adding the split peas, vegetable broth, bay leaf, and thyme. Heat till boiling. (5)Reduce the heat to low and let the peas simmer for forty to forty-five minutes in order to cook them until they are tender. (6)Take off the bay leaf and puree the soup or process it in batches using a standard blender until it's smooth. (7)Taste and add salt and pepper as needed.

SHORTBREAD COOKIES

Total Time: 30 minutes | Prep Time: 10 minutes

Ingredients:

1 cup butter, softened
2 cups all-purpose flour
1 tsp vanilla extract
1/2 cup powdered sugar
1/4 tsp salt

Directions:

(1)Blanch the peas by rinsing them in cool water. (2)Chop the garlic, carrots, onion, and celery finely in a food processor. (3)Saute the chopped veggies in a big saucepan until they're tender. (4)Proceed by adding the split peas, vegetable broth, bay leaf, and thyme. Heat till boiling. (5)Reduce the heat to low and let the peas simmer for forty to forty-five minutes in order to cook them until they are tender. (6)Take off the bay leaf and puree the soup or process it in batches using a standard blender until it's smooth. (7)Taste and add salt and pepper as needed.

ALMOND MACAROONS

Total Time: 30 minutes | Prep Time: 15 minutes

Ingredients:

2 cups shredded coconut
1/2 cup egg whites (about 4 large)
1 cup almond meal
1/2 cup granulated sugar
1/2 tsp almond extract

Directions:

(1)Preheat the oven to 325°F (163°C). Line a baking sheet with parchment paper. (2)In a food processor, blend shredded coconut, almond meal, egg whites, granulated sugar, and almond extract until well mixed. (3)Drop spoonfuls of the mixture onto the prepared baking sheet. (4)Bake for 15-20 minutes or until lightly golden. (5)It should be allowed to cool on the baking sheet before being moved to a wire rack to finish cooling entirely.

CHOCOLATE BUTTER

Total Time: 10 minutes | Prep Time: 10 minutes

Ingredients:

1/2 cup butter, softened
1/4 cup powdered sugar
1/4 cup cocoa powder
1/2 tsp vanilla extract

Directions:

(1)Blend together the butter that has been softened, the cocoa powder, the powdered sugar, and the vanilla extract in a food processor until the mixture is smooth and thoroughly incorporated. The combination should be kept in the refrigerator, and it should be stored in a container that is airtight. Before consuming, allow it to come to room temperature.

RASPBERRY SMOOTHIE

Total Time: 5 minutes | Prep Time: 5 minutes

Ingredients:

1 cup fresh or frozen raspberries
1 cup Greek yogurt
1 banana, peeled
1/2 cup milk (dairy or non-dairy)

1 tablespoon honey or maple syrup (optional)
1/2 teaspoon vanilla extract (optional)

Directions:

(1) Put all of the following ingredients into a food processor: raspberries, banana, yogurt, milk, honey (if you're using it), and vanilla extract (if you're using it at all). (2) Maintain a smooth consistency. (3) Serve the mixture by pouring it into glasses and serving it as quickly as you can once it has been prepared.

CITRUS HERB SPREAD

Total Time: 10 minutes | Prep Time: 10 minutes

Ingredients:

1 cup cream cheese, softened
1 tablespoon fresh orange juice
1 tablespoon fresh chives, chopped
Salt and pepper to taste
2 tablespoons fresh lemon juice
2 tablespoons fresh parsley, chopped
1 teaspoon fresh thyme leaves

Directions:

(1) Use the food processor to combine the following Ingredients: cream cheese, lemon juice, orange juice, parsley, chives, and thyme. (2) Carry out the processing until all of the components are thoroughly mixed and smooth. (3) Salt and pepper should be used to taste, and salt should be used to season. (4) Moving the mixture to a bowl, chill it until you are ready to serve it.

CREAM OF BROCCOLI SOUP

Total Time: 30 minutes | Prep Time: 10 minutes

Ingredients:

1 tablespoon olive oil
2 cloves garlic, minced
2 cups vegetable broth
1 onion, chopped
4 cups broccoli florets
1 cup milk (dairy or non-dairy)
Salt and pepper to taste

Directions:

(1) Olive oil should be heated in a big saucepan over medium heat. Saute the garlic and onion until they are tender. (2) Soup, vegetables, and broccoli should be included. Simmer for approximately 15 minutes, or until broccoli is soft, after bringing to a boil. (3) In small portions, transfer the soup to the food processor and blend until completely smooth. (4) Bring the soup back to a boil. Warm the milk while stirring. Sprinkle with pepper and salt..

SUGAR COOKIES

Total Time: 1 hour | Prep Time: 20 minutes

Ingredients:

1 1/2 cups all-purpose flour
1/4 teaspoon salt
1 cup granulated sugar
1 teaspoon vanilla extract
1/2 teaspoon baking powder
1/2 cup unsalted butter, softened
1 egg

Directions:

(1) Set oven temperature to 350°F, or 175°C. Roll out parchment paper to line baking sheets. (2) Add the salt, baking soda, and flour to the food processor. To combine, pulse. (3) Pulse the food processor with the sugar and butter. Mince till smooth and velvety. (4) Flavour with vanilla extract and egg. Blend everything together. (5) Form dough into balls and set them on baking pans that

have been prepared. Press down using the base of a glass or your palm to make it flat. (6)To get slightly brown edges, bake for 10 to 12 minutes. Return to wire racks to cool..

SPICY VEGAN CHEES

Total Time: 10 minutes | Prep Time: 10 minutes

Ingredients:

1 cup raw cashews	1/4 cup nutritional yeast
1/4 cup water	1/4 cup lemon juice
1 tablespoon tahini	1 garlic clove
1/2 teaspoon smoked paprika	1/4 teaspoon cayenne pepper (adjust to taste)
Salt to taste	

Directions:

(1)All of the components should be placed in the food processor. (2)Additional water is needed in order to achieve the appropriate consistency. Process until smooth and creamy. (3)With the addition of more salt, paprika, or cayenne pepper, the seasoning can be modified to suit your preferences. This can be done according to your preferences.

FRESH BASIL PESTO

Total Time: 10 minutes | Prep Time: 10 minutes

Ingredients:

2 cups fresh basil leaves	1/2 cup pine nuts
1/2 cup grated Parmesan cheese	2 garlic cloves
1/2 cup olive oil	Salt and pepper to taste

Directions:

(1)Garlic, basil, pine nuts, and Parmesan cheese should be added to the food processor. (2)To a finely chopped consistency, process. (3)Meanwhile, while the food processor is operating, gradually incorporate olive oil into the pesto until it achieves the appropriate consistency. (4)Use pepper and salt to season the food.

OATMEAL SMOOTHIE

Total Time: 5 minutes | Prep Time: 5 minutes

Ingredients:

1/2 cup rolled oats	1 banana, peeled
1/2 cup Greek yogurt	1/2 cup milk (dairy or non-dairy)
1 tablespoon honey or maple syrup (optional)	1/2 teaspoon vanilla extract (optional)

Directions:

(1)Utilizing the food processor, include the following Ingredients: oats, banana, yogurt, milk, honey (if used), and vanilla extract (if used). (2)Maintain a smooth consistency. (3)Pour the mixture into glasses and serve it right away.

HAZELNUT SPREAD

Total Time: 15 minutes | Prep Time: 15 minutes

Ingredients:

1 cup roasted hazelnuts, skins removed	1/2 cup powdered sugar
1/4 cup cocoa powder	1/4 cup coconut oil
1/2 teaspoon vanilla extract	A pinch of salt

Directions:

(1) Place hazelnuts in the food processor and process until they turn into a smooth paste. (2) Add powdered sugar, cocoa powder, coconut oil, vanilla extract, and salt. (3) Process until well combined and smooth. (4) Transfer to a jar and store at room temperature.

GARLIC MASHED CAULIFLOWER

Total Time: 20 minutes | Prep Time: 10 minutes

Ingredients:

- 1 large head cauliflower, cut into florets
- 3 cloves garlic, minced
- 1/4 cup unsalted butter or vegan alternative
- 1/4 cup milk (dairy or non-dairy)
- Salt and pepper to taste

Directions:

(1) Steam or boil cauliflower florets until tender, about 10 minutes. (2) Drain well and place in the food processor. (3) Add garlic, butter, and milk to the food processor. (4) Process until smooth and creamy. (5) Season with salt and pepper.

BEET SOUP

Total Time: 45 minutes | Prep Time: 15 minutes

Ingredients:

- 4 medium beets, peeled and diced
- 1 large onion, chopped
- 2 cloves garlic, minced
- 1 large carrot, chopped
- 4 cups vegetable broth
- 2 tbsp olive oil
- 1 tbsp apple cider vinegar
- Salt and pepper to taste
- Fresh dill for garnish (optional)

Directions:

(1) Olive oil should be heated in a big saucepan over medium heat. Toss in the carrot, garlic, and onion. Brown until tender, approximately 5 minutes. (2) After 5 minutes, stir in the beets. (3) Simmer the beets for 25 minutes, or until they are soft, after adding the vegetable broth and bringing to a boil. (4) Separate the soup into batches and pulse in a food processor until completely smooth. Get back into the pot. (5) Toss with the pepper, salt, and apple cider vinegar. Keep it low for another five minutes. (6) If preferred, garnish with fresh dill and serve hot.

CITRUS COMPOTE

Total Time: 20 minutes | Prep Time: 10 minutes

Ingredients:

- 2 oranges, peeled and segmented
- 1 grapefruit, peeled and segmented
- 1 lemon, peeled and segmented
- 2 tbsp honey or maple syruptbsp chopped fresh mint

Directions:

1. Blend the citrus segments with the honey in a food processor until smooth or chunky, according to your preference. If you're using fresh mint, stir it in. Chill it before serving.

CORN FRITTERS

Total Time: 30 minutes | Prep Time: 10 minutes

Ingredients:

- 2 cups corn kernels (fresh or frozen)
- 1/2 cup all-purpose flour
- 1/4 cup cornmeal
- 1/4 cup chopped green onions
- 1 large egg
- 1/4 cup milk

1/2 tsp baking powder 1/4 tsp salt
1/4 tsp black pepper Vegetable oil for frying

1 tbsp maple syrup or 1 tbsp lemon juice\
honey (optional)

Directions:

(1) Blend one cup of corn kernels until they reach a uniform texture in a food processor. Place into a recently scrubbed basin. (2) Combine corn kernels that were set aside, cornmeal, green onions, flour, milk, baking powder, salt, and pepper. Stir in the egg. (3) Grease a skillet and set it over medium heat. Flatten the batter slightly before dropping spoonfuls into the skillet. Settle in for approximately 3 minutes on each side or until a golden brown color develops. (4) Place a paper towel over the drained area and serve heat.

Directions:

(1) The recommended temperature for flax milk is 110 degrees Fahrenheit (43 degrees Celsius), which can be achieved by heating it in a pot over medium heat. Take away from the heat. (2) Add plain yogurt and honey or maple syrup, if using, and stir until combined. (3) To allow the mixture to ferment, cover it and place it in a warm place for eight to twelve hours. (4) After stirring in the lemon juice, place the mixture in the refrigerator for approximately twelve hours or until it has thickened.

LEMON GARLIC AIOLI

Total Time: 10 minutes | Prep Time: 10 minutes

Ingredients:

1 cup mayonnaise 3 cloves garlic, minced
Zest and juice of 1 lemon 1 tbsp olive oil
Salt and pepper to taste

Directions:

(1) Mayonnaise, garlic, lemon zest, lemon juice, and olive oil should be the ingredients that are combined in a food processor. (2) Mix until it is completely smooth and properly blended. (3) Add salt and pepper to taste, and season with salt. (4) Before serving, chill the food.

FLAX MILK YOGURT

Total Time: 24 hours | Prep Time: 10 minutes

Ingredients:

4 cups flax milk 2 tbsp plain yogurt
(with live cultures)

ALMOND ENERGY BALLS

Total Time: 15 minutes | Prep Time: 15 minutes

Ingredients:

1 cup almonds 1 cup pitted dates
1/4 cup unsweetened 1 tbsp chia seeds
cocoa powder
1 tbsp honey or maple
syrup

Directions:

(1) Almonds should be pounded into a fine powder in a food processor. Dates, cocoa powder, chia seeds, and honey should then be added to the mixture and processed until it comes together. The mixture can then be rolled into small balls and placed in the refrigerator until it becomes firm.

SOY MILK CHEESE

Total Time: 3-4 hours | Prep Time: 10 minutes

Ingredients:

2 cups soy milk	1/4 cup lemon juice or vinegar
1/2 tsp salt	1/4 cup nutritional yeast (optional)

Directions:

(1)Bring the soy milk to a simmer in a saucepan. Get it out of the oven. (2)Before letting it sit for 10 minutes to curdle, stir in the vinegar or lemon juice. (3)After the milk has curdled, strain it through a cheesecloth-lined sieve. Set aside to drain for at least one and a half hours. (4)If using nutritional yeast, combine it with the salt.

Chill before consuming.

SAFFLOWER CHEESE

Total Time: 3-4 hours | Prep Time: 10 minutes

Ingredients:

2 cups safflower milk	1/4 cup lemon juice or vinegar
1/2 tsp salt	1/4 cup nutritional yeast (optional)

Directions:

(1)Bring safflower milk to a simmer in a saucepan. Get it out of the oven. (2)Before letting it sit for 10 minutes to curdle, stir in the vinegar or lemon juice. (3)After the milk has curdled, strain it through a cheesecloth-lined sieve. Set aside to drain for at least one and a half hours. (4)If using nutritional yeast, combine it with the salt. (5)Chill before consuming.

CREAMY AVOCADO DRESSING

Total Time: 10 minutes | Prep Time: 10 minutes

Ingredients:

2 ripe avocados	1/4 cup lemon juice
1/4 cup olive oil	1 clove garlic
1/4 cup fresh cilantro (optional)	Salt and pepper to taste

Directions:

(1)Use a food processor to combine the avocados, lemon juice, olive oil, garlic, and cilantro (if desired) until everything is evenly distributed. (2)Blend until it is completely smooth. (3)Add salt and pepper to taste, and season with salt. (4)Before serving, chill the food.

SOY MILK YOGURT

Total Time: 24 hours (including fermentation) | Prep Time: 10 minutes

Ingredients:

4 cups soy milk	2 tbsp plain soy yogurt (with live cultures)
1 tbsp maple syrup or honey (optional)	1 tbsp lemon juice

Directions:

(1)Bring the soy milk to a boil in a saucepan over medium heat, then reduce heat to low and simmer for 10 minutes. Heat the stovetop to low. (2)Add unflavored soy yogurt and, if desired, maple syrup or honey. (3)Cover and let sit in a warm place for 8-12 hours to ferment. (4)Stir in lemon juice and refrigerate until thickened about 12 hours.

SPINACH ARTICHOKE DIP

Total Time: 20 minutes | Prep Time: 10 minutes

Ingredients:

2 cups fresh spinach,	1 can (14 oz) artichoke

chopped

1 cup sour cream

1 cup grated Parmesan cheese

2 cloves garlic, minced

1/4 teaspoon black pepper

hearts, drained and chopped

1 cup mayonnaise

1 cup shredded mozzarella cheese

1/2 teaspoon salt

Directions:

(1) The oven should be preheated to a temperature of 190 degrees Celsius (375 degrees Fahrenheit). (2) Blend together artichoke hearts, spinach, sour cream, mayonnaise, mozzarella, Parmesan, garlic, salt, and pepper in a food processor. (3) Blend until blended and completely smooth. (4) After the mixture has been transferred, spread it out in a uniform layer in a baking dish. (5) Before the top begins to bubble and turn golden, bake for 20 minutes. (6) Accompany with toast or crackers while hot.

FRESH HERB BUTTER

Total Time: 10 minutes | Prep Time: 10 minutes

Ingredients:

1 cup unsalted butter, softened

2 tablespoons fresh chives, chopped

1 clove garlic, minced

1/4 teaspoon black pepper

2 tablespoons fresh parsley, chopped

2 tablespoons fresh basil, chopped

1/2 teaspoon salt

Directions:

(1) Put the butter that has been softened into a food processor. (2) Mix in some garlic, parsley, chives, basil, and salt & pepper to taste. (3) It is important to process the herbs until they are finely chopped and thoroughly integrated into the butter. (4) Place in a container and chill in the refrigerator until it becomes solid. (5) Utilize as a spread or to boost the flavor of foods.

CREAMY SALSA VERDE

Total Time: 10 minutes | Prep Time: 10 minutes

Ingredients:

1 cup tomatillos, husked and chopped

1/4 cup chopped onion

1 clove garlic

Juice of 1 lime

1/2 cup fresh cilantro leaves

1 jalapeño, seeded and chopped

1/2 teaspoon salt

Directions:

(1) Utilize a food processor to combine the following Ingredients: tomatillos, cilantro, onion, jalapeño, garlic, salt, and lime juice. (2) Until the mixture is silky smooth and creamy. (3) Test the seasoning, then make any required adjustments. (4) Serve as a dip, with tacos, or with meats that have been grilled.

CREAMY CAULIFLOWER SAUCE

Total Time: 20 minutes | Prep Time: 10 minutes

Ingredients:

1 head cauliflower, chopped into florets

1 cup vegetable broth

1/4 cup plain Greek yogurt

1/4 teaspoon black pepper

2 cloves garlic, minced

1/2 cup nutritional yeast

1/2 teaspoon salt

Directions:

1. After roughly 10 minutes of steaming, the cauliflower florets should be soft. (2)The steamed cauliflower, garlic, veggie broth, nutritional yeast, Greek yogurt, salt, and pepper should all be mixed together in a food processor. (3)Beat in the cream until completely combined. (2)Salt and pepper to taste. (3)If you're looking for a creamy topping, veggie dip, or spaghetti dish, this is it!.

SPINACH SOUP

Total Time: 30 minutes | Prep Time: 15 minutes

Ingredients:

4 cups fresh spinach	1 onion, chopped
2 cloves garlic, minced	4 cups vegetable broth
1 cup milk (or plant-based milk)	1 tablespoon olive oil
1/2 teaspoon salt	1/4 teaspoon black pepper

Directions:

(1)Slowly bring olive oil to a simmer in a big saucepan. (2)Reduce heat to low and sauté garlic and onion until softened. (3)Before boiling, add the veggie broth. (4)Cook the spinach until it wilts, then add it. (5)Place in a food processor and pulse until completely smooth. (6)Stir in the milk, salt, and pepper, then return to the pot and cook until heated through. (7)Heat and serve immediately.

MINT CHOCOLATE ENERGY BALLS

Total Time: 15 minutes | Prep Time: 15 minutes

Ingredients:

1 cup pitted dates	1 cup almonds
1/2 cup cocoa powder	1/4 cup unsweetened shredded coconut
1 tablespoon fresh mint leaves	1 tablespoon chia seeds
1/4 teaspoon vanilla extract	

Directions:

(1)Mint leaves, chia seeds, dates, almonds, cocoa powder, coconut, and vanilla extract should all be mixed together in a food processor. (2)Finely grind the ingredients in a food processor until the mixture clumps together when squeezed. (3)Form into little balls with the mixture and chill for at least 15 minutes before serving. (4)Place in a refrigerator-safe container and seal tightly.

VEGGIE FRITTERS

Total Time: 30 minutes | Prep Time: 15 minutes

Ingredients:

1 cup grated zucchini, squeezed to remove excess moisture	1 cup grated carrots
1/2 cup finely chopped onion	1/2 cup flour
1/2 cup grated Parmesan cheese	2 eggs, beaten
1/2 teaspoon salt	1/4 teaspoon black pepper
Olive oil for frying	

Directions:

(1)Mixed together in a big basin are the following Ingredients: zucchini, carrots, onion, flour, Parmesan cheese, eggs, pepper, and salt. (2)Combine by mixing thoroughly. (3)Following the transfer of the mixture, it should be spread out in a baking dish in a layer that is homogeneous throughout. (4)It is recommended that the mixture be added to the pan in spoonfuls, and then the back of the spoon should be used to press down on the mixture in order to make it roughly flat. (5)About three to four minutes per side, cook until golden brown. (6)Place the food in a dish that has been lined with paper towels in order to remove any extra grease that may be present. (7)Warm it up and serve it as a side, or dunk it in some sauce.

STRAWBERRY ENERGY BALLS

Total Time: 15 minutes | Prep Time: 15 minutes

Ingredients:

1 cup dried strawberries	1 cup almonds
1/2 cup oats	2 tablespoons honey
1 tablespoon chia seeds	1/4 teaspoon vanilla extract

Directions:

(1)Blend together the oats, almonds, honey, chia seeds, and vanilla extract with the dried strawberries in a food processor. (2)The mixture should be processed until it begins to come together and is finely chopped. (3)Form into little balls with the mixture and chill for at least 15 minutes before serving. (4)Place in a refrigerator-safe container and seal tightly.

PEANUT BUTTER SPREAD

Total Time: 10 minutes | Prep Time: 10 minutes

Ingredients:

2 cups roasted peanuts	1/4 cup peanut oil (or more as needed)
1/4 teaspoon salt	tablespoons honey (optional)

Directions:

(1)Toss the peanuts into a grinder. (2)Pulse the peanuts until they become a coarse pulp. (3)While processing, gradually drizzle in peanut oil until spread consistency is achieved. (4)Puree till smooth, then add honey and salt, if using. (5)Spoon into a jar and set aside to cool or refrigerate.

BERRY SMOOTHIE

Total Time: 5 minutes | Prep Time: 5 minutes

Ingredients:

1 cup mixed berries (fresh or frozen)	1 banana
1 cup spinach (optional)	1 cup almond milk (or any milk)
1 tablespoon honey (optional)	

Directions:

(1)Blending or using a food processor to combine berries, bananas, spinach (if used), almond milk, and honey is the recommended method. Blend or process until smooth. (2)The mixture should be brought to the point where it is fully smooth and creamy. (3)Serve the mixture by pouring it into glasses and serving it as quickly as you can once it has been prepared.

PECAN BUTTER

Total Time: 10 minutes | Prep Time: 10 minutes

Ingredients:

2 cups pecans	1/4 tsp salt
1-2 tbsp maple syrup or honey (optional for sweetness)	

Directions:

(1)Get the food processor going with the pecans. (2)To make a nice meal out of pecans, process them on high until they break down. (3)When necessary, scrape the edges of the dish. (4)For another five to seven minutes, or until the pecans are ground into a butter consistency, continue processing. (5)Process once more to blend with salt and, if preferred, maple syrup or honey. (6)You may keep it in the fridge for up to a month or at room temperature for up to two weeks if you seal it tightly.

PISTACHIO ENERGY BALLS

Total Time: 15 minutes | Prep Time: 15 minutes

Ingredients:

1 cup raw pistachios	1 cup dates, pitted
1/2 cup shredded coconut	1 tbsp chia seeds
1 tbsp hemp seeds	1/2 tsp vanilla extract

Directions:

(1)To make fine crumbs, pulse the pistachios in a food processor. (2)Mix in the dates, coconut shreds, chia seeds, hemp seeds, and vanilla essence. (3)Blend or process until a dough forms that holds its shape when squeezed. (4)Shape the mixture into balls using tablespoons. (5)You may keep it in the fridge for up to two weeks if you seal it.

MANGO SALSA

Total Time: 10 minutes | Prep Time: 10 minute

Ingredients:

1 ripe mango, peeled and diced	1/2 red onion, finely chopped
1/2 red bell pepper, diced	1/4 cup fresh cilantro, chopped
1 lime, juiced	Salt to taste

Directions:

(1)The mango, red onion, red bell pepper, and cilantro should be pulsed in a food processor a few times in order to achieve a smoother consistency. (2)Toss the lime juice and salt into the mixture after transferring it to a dish. Try it out and make any necessary adjustments to the flavor. You can serve it right away, or you can put it in the refrigerator for up to two days.

PUMPKIN PIE ENERGY BALLS

Total Time: 15 minutes | Prep Time: 15 minutes

Ingredients:

1 cup raw almonds	1/2 cup pumpkin puree
1/2 cup dates, pitted	1/4 cup pumpkin seeds
1 tbsp maple syrup	1 tsp pumpkin pie spice
Pinch of salt	

Directions:

(1)Utilizing a food processor, grind the almonds into a very fine powder. (2)Include pumpkin pie spice, dates, pumpkin seeds, maple syrup, and pumpkin puree. (3)Mix until everything is mixed and forms a cohesive mass when squeezed. (4)Shape the mixture into balls using tablespoons.

FERMENTED NUT CHEESE

Total Time: 48 hours | Prep Time: 15 minutes

Ingredients:

1 cup raw cashews (soaked for 4 hours)	2 tbsp nutritional yeast
1/4 cup water	2 tbsp lemon juice
1/4 cup coconut oil (melted)	1/2 tsp salt

1/4 tsp probiotic powder (from probiotic capsules)
1 tbsp chopped fresh herbs (optional)

Directions:

(1)After soaking the cashews, drain and rinse them. (2)Raw cashews, nutritional yeast, coconut oil, salt, lemon juice, and water should all be mixed together in a food processor. Beat in the cream until completely combined. (3)Mix with the powdered probiotic. (4)Fill a jar or other container with the mixture and cover it loosely with cheesecloth or a lid. (5)Allow the ingredients to ferment for at least a day or two at room temperature. Its sourness is proportional to the time it spends fermenting. (6)Add fresh herbs if you like after fermentation, then put them in the fridge. It has a two-week shelf life in the fridge.

CINNAMON BUTTER

Total Time: 10 minutes | Prep Time: 10 minutes

Ingredients:

1 cup unsalted butter (softened)
1/4 cup powdered sugar
1/2 tsp ground cinnamon
1/2 tsp vanilla extract

Directions:

(1)Put softened butter, powdered sugar, cinnamon, and vanilla essence into a food processor and mix them together. (2)The mixture should be processed until it is silky, smooth, and creamy. (3)Place it in a container, and then put it in the refrigerator to keep it fresh. Before distributing it, you should wait until it has reached room temperature.

VEGETABLE SOUP

Total Time: 45 minutes | Prep Time: 15 minutes

Ingredients:

1 tbsp olive oil
1 large onion, chopped
2 cloves garlic, minced
3 carrots, peeled and chopped
2 celery stalks, chopped
1 bell pepper, chopped
1 cup green beans, chopped
4 cups vegetable broth
1 can (15 oz) diced tomatoes
1 tsp dried thyme
1 tsp dried basil
Salt and pepper to taste

Directions:

(1)Olive oil should be heated in a big saucepan over medium heat. (2)Reduce heat to low and sauté garlic and onion until softened. (3)Prepare the vegetables by adding green beans, carrots, celery, and bell pepper. Allow to cook for a further five minutes. (4)Add the veggie stock and chopped tomatoes. Add basil and thyme and mix well. (5)After the vegetables are soft, about 25 to 30 minutes after bringing them to a boil, reduce heat and simmer. (6)Taste and add salt and pepper as needed. Heat and serve immediately.

CARROT FRITTERS

Total Time: 30 minutes | Prep Time: 15 minutes

Ingredients:

2 cups grated carrots
1/2 cup finely chopped onion
1/4 cup all-purpose flour
1/4 cup grated Parmesan cheese
1 large egg
1/2 tsp baking powder
1/2 tsp ground cumin
Salt and pepper to taste
Olive oil for frying

Directions:

(1)Pulverize the chopped carrots and onion with the flour, Parmesan cheese, egg, baking powder, cumin, salt, and pepper in a food processor. Blend until combined. (2)In a skillet set over medium heat, warm a thin layer of olive oil. (3)Flatten spoonfuls of the mixture into fritters in the skillet. (4)For a golden finish, cook for two to three minutes on each side. (5)Brown and crispy. (6)Drain on paper towels before serving.

SUN-DRIED TOMATO SPREAD

Total Time: 10 minutes | Prep Time: 10 minutes

Ingredients:

- 1 cup sun-dried tomatoes
- 2 cloves garlic
- 1 tbsp lemon juice
- 1/4 cup walnuts
- 2 tbsp olive oil
- Salt and pepper to taste

Directions:

(1)Put walnuts, sun-dried tomatoes, garlic, olive oil, and lemon juice in a food processor. (2)Blend the ingredients until they are completely smooth, pausing to scrape down the sides if required. (3)Taste and add salt and pepper as needed. (4)Pour into a jar and refrigerate until needed. You can store it for up to two weeks. (5)Of course! In order to make everything you mentioned in a food processor, I have included the detailed recipes here.

VEGAN CREAM CHEESE

Total Time: 15 minutes | Prep Time: 15 minutes

Ingredients:

- 1 cup raw cashews, soaked in water for at least 2 hours
- 1/4 cup water
- 1/4 cup lemon juice
- 1 garlic clove
- 1/2 teaspoon onion powder (optional)
- 1/4 cup nutritional yeast
- 1/2 teaspoon salt
- 1/4 teaspoon turmeric (optional, for color)

Directions:

(1)After the cashews have soaked, drain and rinse them. In a food processor, combine the cashews, water, nutritional yeast, lemon juice, garlic, salt, and any optional ingredients. (2)Pulse until smooth and creamy, stopping to scrape down the sides as needed. Season to taste. When ready to serve, transfer to a container and chill for at least an hour to thicken.

ARTICHOKE PARMESAN DIP

Total Time: 10 minutes | Prep Time: 10 minutes

Ingredients

- 1 can (14 oz) artichoke hearts, drained
- 1/4 cup nutritional yeast
- 1 tablespoon lemon juice
- 1/2 teaspoon salt
- 1/4 cup water (or more as needed)
- 1/2 cup raw cashews
- 1/4 cup vegan Parmesan cheese
- 1 garlic clove
- 1/4 teaspoon black pepper

Directions:

1.of the ingredients should be placed in a food processor and processed until they are completely mixed together. (2)Add water little by little until the mixture reaches the consistency you want. Taste it and add more seasoning if needed. Serve right away or store in the fridge until needed.

MACADAMIA NUT BUTTER

Total Time: 10 minutes | Prep Time: 10 minutes

Ingredients:

2 cups raw macadamia nuts
1-2 tablespoons neutral oil (optional for smoother texture)1.

1/4 teaspoon salt (optional)

Throw the macadamia nuts into the blender. (2)Pulse rapidly, stopping to scrape down sides as needed. (3)To make it creamier, you can add salt and oil if you want.

There will be a progression from coarse meal to thick paste to creamy butter as the nuts are processed.

CHIA SEED ENERGY BALLS

Total Time: 15 minutes | Prep Time: 15 minutes

Ingredients:

1 cup pitted dates
1/4 cup chia seeds
2 tablespoons cocoa powder or carob powder (optional)

1/2 cup raw almonds
1/4 cup shredded coconut
1 tablespoon maple syrup or honey (optional)

Directions:

(1)Place dates and almonds in the food processor and pulse until finely chopped. (2)Add chia seeds, shredded coconut, and cocoa powder (if using). Process until well combined. (3)Taste the mixture and add maple syrup or honey if additional sweetness is desired. (4)The mixture should be rolled into little balls with a diameter of approximately one inch. (5)Refrigerate for at least 30 minutes to set. Ensure that the container is sealed and place it in the refrigerator. Cream of

ASPARAGUS SOUP

Total Time: 30 minutes | Prep Time: 15 minutes

Ingredients:

1 bunch asparagus, trimmed and cut into pieces
1 onion, chopped
2 cups vegetable broth
Salt and pepper to taste

1 tablespoon olive oil
2 garlic cloves, minced
1/2 cup coconut milk
1 tablespoon lemon juice (optional)

Directions:

(1)Slowly bring olive oil to a simmer in a big saucepan. Reduce heat to low and sauté garlic and onion until softened. (2)While stirring occasionally, simmer the asparagus for 5 minutes. (3)Toss the veggies into the preheated dish after boiling the liquid. Simmer, covered, for 10 minutes or until asparagus reaches desired tenderness. (4)Put the mixture of asparagus and onions into the food processor using a slotted spoon. Blend in the coconut milk until it's completely smooth. (5)Before heating completely, add the combined ingredients back to the pot. To taste, add fresh lemon juice, salt, and pepper. (6)Heat and serve immediately.

COCONUT MILK CHEESE

Total Time: 6 hours | Prep Time: 15 minutes

Ingredients:

1 cup coconut milk (full-fat)
2 tbsp lemon juice
1/2 tsp salt

1/4 cup nutritional yeast
1 tbsp agar-agar powder
1/4 tsp garlic powder (optional)

Directions:

(1)Coconut milk should be heated in a saucepan over medium heat. (2)Add the agar-agar powder and stir while the mixture begins to boil. (3)Maintain a steady stirring motion while bringing the mixture to a simmer over low heat for one or two minutes. (4)Whisk in the nutritional yeast, salt, lemon juice, and garlic powder (if using) after taking it off the heat. (5)Once combined, transfer to a container or mold and chill for at least four hours or until solid.

STRAWBERRY CHOCOLATE SPREAD

Total Time: 10 minutes | Prep Time: 10 minutes

Ingredients:

1 cup strawberries, hulled	1/2 cup dark chocolate chips
2 tbsp maple syrup	1/2 tsp vanilla extract

Directions:

(1)Blend the dark chocolate chips by melting them in a microwave or double boiler. (2)Make a puree of the strawberries by blending them in a food processor. (3)Put the maple syrup, vanilla extract, melted chocolate, and maple syrup into the food processor. (4)Mix everything together until it's completely smooth. (5)Put in the fridge until you're ready to use it.

CASHEW CHEESE

Total Time: 4 hours | Prep Time: 10 minutes

Ingredients:

1 cup raw cashews (soaked for at least 2 hours)	1/4 cup nutritional yeast
2 tbsp lemon juice	1/4 cup water
1/2 tsp garlic powder	1/4 tsp turmeric (for color, optional)
1/4 tsp salt	

Directions:

(1)After soaking the cashews, drain and rinse them. (2)Bring all the ingredients to a boil in a food processor: cashews, nutritional yeast, water, garlic powder, turmeric (if desired), and salt. (3)With occasional scraping of the sides, blend until a creamy consistency is achieved. (4)Transfer to a container after seasoning to taste. (5)Put in the fridge for at least two hours to set before serving.

GAZPACHO

Total Time: 30 minutes | Prep Time: 15 minutes

Ingredients:

4 ripe tomatoes, chopped	1 cucumber, peeled and chopped
1 bell pepper, chopped	1 small red onion, chopped
2 cloves garlic, minced	1/4 cup red wine vinegar
1/4 cup olive oil	Salt and pepper to taste
Fresh basil or parsley for garnish	

Directions:

(1)Throw the garlic, red onion, cucumber, bell pepper, and tomatoes into a food processor. (2)Combine ingredients and mix until creamy. (3)Blend in the olive oil and red wine vinegar once more. (4)If necessary, season with salt and pepper. (5)Please put it in the fridge and let it chill for at least two hours before you serve it. (6)Add a sprinkle of parsley or basil for garnish.

CREAMY TOMATO SOUP

Total Time: 40 minutes | Prep Time: 10 minutes

Ingredients:

1 tbsp olive oil
2 cloves garlic, minced
1 cup vegetable broth
1 tsp dried basil
1 onion, chopped
2 cans (15 oz each) diced tomatoes
1/2 cup coconut milk
Salt and pepper to taste

Directions:

(1)Heat the olive oil in a big saucepan over medium heat until it melts. (2)Cook the garlic and onion, tossing them around occasionally until they start to soften. (3)Then, stir in the dried basil, vegetable broth, and diced tomatoes. (4)After the mixture boils, lower the heat and simmer for twenty minutes. (5)If you don't have an immersion blender, use a standard blender in batches to puree the soup. (6)Mix in the coconut milk with a little salt and pepper. (7)Finish heating before you eat.

PROTEIN SMOOTHIE

Total Time: 5 minutes | Prep Time: 5 minutes

Ingredients:

1 cup almond milk
1 scoop protein powder
1 tsp honey (optional)
1/2 cup frozen berries
1 tbsp chia seeds

Directions:

(1)Put everything in a blender and blend until smooth. (2)Process until the mixture is totally smooth. (3)Serve immediately by pouring the mixture into a glass.

ARTICHOKE SPREAD

Total Time: 10 minutes | Prep Time: 10 minutes

Ingredients:

1 can (14 oz) artichoke hearts, drained
1/4 cup grated Parmesan cheese
1 tbsp lemon juice
1/4 cup mayonnaise
2 cloves garlic, minced
Salt and pepper to taste

Directions:

(1)With the use of a food processor, combine the artichoke hearts, mayonnaise, Parmesan cheese, garlic, and lemon juice. Process the mixture until it is completely blended. (2)Blend until it is completely smooth. (3)Salt and pepper should be used to taste, and salt should be used to season. (4)It can be served right away, or it can be stored in the refrigerator until it is required.

CINNAMON ENERGY BALLS

Total Time: 10 minutes | Prep Time: 10 minutes

Ingredients:

1 cup rolled oats
1/4 cup honey
1 tsp ground cinnamon
1/2 cup almond butter
1/4 cup ground flaxseeds
1/4 cup mini chocolate chips (optional)

Directions:

(1)Make sure that all of the ingredients are thoroughly blended in a bowl. (2)The ingredients should be rolled into little balls. (3)Please put it in the refrigerator for half an hour to allow it to set before serving.

BLUEBERRY ENERGY BALLS

Total Time: 10 minutes| Prep Time: 10 minutes

Ingredients:

1 cup rolled oats
1/4 cup honey
1/2 cup cashew butter
1/2 cup dried blueberries

1/4 cup chia seeds

Directions:

(1) Make sure that all of the ingredients are thoroughly blended in a bowl. (2) Roll the mixture into small balls. (3) Refrigerate for 30 minutes to firm up before serving.

BLUEBERRY LEMON SPREAD

Total Time: 15 minutes | Prep Time: 15 minutes

Ingredients:

1 cup fresh or frozen blueberries
1/4 cup maple syrup
1/2 tsp vanilla extract
1/4 cup lemon juice
1 tbsp cornstarch

Directions:

(1) Heat the mixture after combining the blueberries, lemon juice, and maple syrup in a saucepan. (2) Prepare the blueberries over medium heat until they exude their juices. (3) The cornstarch should be combined with a small amount of water and then stirred into the blueberry mixture. (4) Cook for around five to seven minutes or until the mixture has thickened. (5) After taking the pan off the heat, whisk in the vanilla extract. (6) Let it cool down before transferring it to a jar or other container.

LENTIL PATTIES

Total Time: 45 minutes | Prep Time: 15 minutes

Ingredients:

1 cup dried lentils
1 small onion, chopped
1 carrot, grated
1 teaspoon ground cumin
1/2 teaspoon salt
1/2 cup breadcrumbs (or gluten-free alternative)
2 cups water
2 cloves garlic, minced
1/4 cup fresh parsley, chopped
1 teaspoon smoked paprika
1/4 teaspoon black pepper
2 tablespoons olive oil

Directions:

(1) Lentils should be boiled in water for around 20 minutes after rinsing them. Set aside to cool. (2) Add the lentils, garlic, carrot, parsley, cumin, paprika, salt, and pepper to a food processor. Chop until smooth. Toss in the ingredients and pulse until they are finely minced but not smooth. (3) After a few more pulses, add the breadcrumbs and mix well. (4) Form patties with the mixture. (5) Prepare the olive oil by heating it in a skillet that is set over medium heat. Fry patties for three to four minutes per side or until they get a golden brown color.

BANANA LENTIL PATTIES

Total Time: 50 minutes | Prep Time: 15 minutes

Ingredients:

1 cup dried lentils
1 large ripe banana
2 cloves garlic, minced
1 teaspoon ground coriander
1/2 teaspoon salt
1/2 cup oat flour
2 cups water
1 small onion, chopped
1/4 cup fresh cilantro, chopped
1 teaspoon turmeric
1/4 teaspoon black pepper
2 tablespoons coconut oil

Directions:

(1)Lentils should be boiled in water for around 20 minutes after rinsing them. Set aside to cool. (2)Add the lentils, garlic, carrot, parsley, cumin, paprika, salt, and pepper to a food processor. Chop until smooth. Toss in the ingredients and pulse until they are finely minced but not smooth. (3)After a few more pulses, add the breadcrumbs and mix well. (4)Form patties with the mixture. (5)Prepare the olive oil by heating it in a skillet that is set over medium heat. Fry patties for three to four minutes per side or until they get a golden brown color.

BANANA OAT COOKIES

Total Time: 30 minutes | Prep Time: 10 minutes

Ingredients:

2 ripe bananas
1/2 cup almond butter
1/2 teaspoon cinnamon
1/2 cup dark chocolate chips (optional)
1 1/2 cups rolled oats
1/4 cup maple syrup
1/4 teaspoon salt

Directions:

(1)When you have your oven preheated at 350 degrees Fahrenheit (175 degrees Celsius), prepare a baking sheet by lining it with parchment paper. (2)A smooth consistency should be achieved by mashing the bananas. (3)Grind the almonds and mix them with the maple syrup, cinnamon, salt, and oats. Blend everything. (4)If using, stir in the chocolate chips. (5)The dough should be dropped onto the prepared baking sheet in a heaping spoonful, and then a slight amount of pressure should be applied. (6)To get golden brown cookies, bake for around fifteen to twenty minutes.

HASH BROWNS

Total Time: 30 minutes | Prep Time: 10 minutes

Ingredients:

4 medium potatoes, peeled and grated
2 tablespoons flour
1/4 teaspoon black pepper
1 small onion, grated
1 teaspoon salt
2 tablespoons olive oil

Directions:

(1)After grating the potatoes and onion, please place them in a clean cloth and press out any extra moisture. (2)Potatoes, onion, flour, pepper, salt, and food processor should be mixed together. Blend until combined. (3)In a skillet set over medium heat, warm the olive oil. (4)Cook the potato mixture patties for three to four minutes per side or until they are crispy and a golden brown color.

VEGAN FETA

Total Time: 15 minutes | Prep Time: 10 minutes

Ingredients:

1 block firm tofu, drained and pressed
2 tablespoons lemon juice
1 tablespoon olive oil
1/2 teaspoon salt
1/4 cup nutritional yeast
2 tablespoons apple cider vinegar
1 teaspoon dried oregano
1/4 teaspoon garlic powder

Directions:

(1)Puree the tofu in a food processor. (2)Include nutritional yeast, olive oil, oregano, salt, garlic powder, lemon juice, and apple cider vinegar. Blend everything together until smooth. (3)Put in the fridge for at least an hour to allow flavors to combine after transferring to a container. \

MAPLE SYRUP YOGURT

Total Time: 5 minutes | Prep Time: 5 minutes

Ingredients:

2 cups plain non-dairy yogurt
1 teaspoon vanilla extract
1/4 cup maple syrup

Directions:

(1)In a bowl, combine yogurt, maple syrup, and vanilla extract. (2)Stir until well mixed. (3)Serve immediately, or store in the refrigerator until you are needed.

CARAMEL SPREAD

Total Time: 20 minutes | PreOp Time: 10 minutes

Ingredients:

1 cup dates, pitted
1/4 cup maple syrup
Pinch of salt
1/4 cup almond butter
1/2 teaspoon vanilla extract

Directions:

(1)Dates should be soaked in warm water for ten minutes before being drained. (2)Blend dates in a food processor until they are completely smooth. (3)Add salt, maple syrup, vanilla essence, and almond butter to the mixture. Mix until everything is incorporated and creamy. (4)Replace in a jar and place in the refrigerator.

MOCHA ENERGY BALLS

Total Time: 15 minutes | Prep Time: 10 minutes

Ingredients:

1 cup pitted dates
1/4 cup cocoa powder
1/4 cup shredded coconut (optional)
1/2 cup almonds
1/4 cup espresso or strong coffee
Pinch of salt

Directions:

(1)To achieve a finely chopped consistency, the dates and almonds should be processed in a food processor until they reach optimal consistency. (2)Powdered cocoa, espresso, and salt should be added. Process the mixture until it can be held together when it is squeezed. (3)You can coat the mixture with shredded coconut if you so wish after rolling it into little balls. (4)Put it in the refrigerator.

CHIA SEED JAM

Total Time: 10 minutes | Prep Time: 10 minutes

Ingredients:

2 cups fresh or frozen berries
2 2 tablespoons chia seeds
1 tablespoons maple syrup
1 tablespoon lemon juice

Directions:

(1)Make sure that the berries and maple syrup are heated together in a pot over medium heat until the berries begin to separate. (2)Berries can be mashed with a spoon or a fork. (3)The chia seeds and lemon juice should be mixed in. Continue to cook for a further five minutes while tossing the mixture often. (4)Before transferring to a jar, allow it to cool down. Bring to a close.

VEGAN CHEESE SPREAD

Total Time: 10 minutes | Prep Time: 10 minutes

Ingredients:

- 1/2 cup cashews, soaked and drained
- 1/4 cup water
- 1 garlic clove
- 1/4 cup nutritional yeast
- 2 tablespoons lemon juice
- 1/2 teaspoon salt

Directions:

(1) Combine all of the ingredients in a food processor and pulse until the mixture is smooth and creamy. (2) Adjust the seasoning to your liking. (3) Place in a jar, and then place in the refrigerator.

ROASTED PEPPER SPREAD

Total Time: 25 minutes | Prep Time: 10 minutes

Ingredients:

- 2 large red bell peppers
- 1/4 cup walnuts
- 2 cloves garlic
- 2 tablespoons olive oil
- 1 tablespoon lemon juice
- 1/2 teaspoon smoked paprika
- Salt and pepper to taste

Directions:

(1) Cook for a minimum of 10 minutes in a preheated oven of 450 F (230 C). For 20 minutes, toss the peppers every so often, roasting them in the oven until the skins become black. (2) Simmer the peppers for 10 minutes with the lid on. Extract the seeds by peeling off the skins. (3) Combine all of the ingredients in a food processor and pulse until smooth. Add garlic, walnuts, olive oil, lemon juice, smoked paprika, salt, and pepper. (4) Put it into a jar and put it in the fridge.

THAI PEANUT DIP

Total Time: 10 minutes | Prep Time: 10 minutes

Ingredients:

- 1 cup creamy peanut butter
- 2 tbsp honey
- 1 tbsp sesame oil
- 1 tsp fresh ginger, grated
- 1/4 cup soy sauce
- 2 tbsp rice vinegar
- 1 clove garlic, minced
- 1/4 cup water (more as needed)

Directions:

(1) Get all the ingredients—ginger, garlic, peanut butter, rice vinegar, soy sauce, honey, and sesame oil—pulsed together. (2) Whip till completely smooth. (3) You can adjust the consistency by adding water a spoonful at a time. (4) Pair with crisp greens or use as a spring roll dip.

HONEY YOGURT

Total Time: 5 minutes | Prep Time: 5 minutes

Ingredients:

- 2 cups Greek yogurt
- 1 tsp vanilla extract (optional)
- 2 tbsp honey

Directions:

(1) In a bowl, combine Greek yogurt and honey. (2) Stir until well mixed. (3) Add vanilla extract if using. (4) Serve immediately or refrigerate for later use.

COCONUT ENERGY BALLS

Total Time: 10 minutes | Prep Time: 10 minutes

Ingredients:

- 1 cup shredded coconut
- 1/2 cup almonds
- 1 tbsp coconut oil
- 1 cup pitted dates
- 2 tbsp cocoa powder

Directions:

(1) A food processor should be used to combine shredded coconut, dates, almonds, cocoa powder, and coconut oil, among other ingredients. (2) Process the combination until it is finely chopped, and a cohesive consistency is achieved when it is mashed together. (3) Form the mixture into tiny balls using your hands. (4) Ensure that the dish is chilled for at least half an hour before serving.

KALE SMOOTHIE

Total Time: 5 minutes | Prep Time: 5 minutes

Ingredients:

- 1 cup kale leaves, stems removed
- 1/2 cup almond milk (or other milk of choice)
- 1 tbsp chia seeds (optional)
- 1 banana
- 1/2 cup frozen pineapple chunks

Directions:

(1) Within a blender, combine the chia seeds, banana, almond milk, pineapple pieces, and greens. Blend until smooth. (2) Blend until it is completely smooth. (3) Pour the mixture into glasses and serve it right away.

CAULIFLOWER SOUP

Total Time: 30 minutes | Prep Time: 10 minutes

Ingredients:

- 1 large head of cauliflower, chopped
- 2 cloves garlic, minced
- 1 cup coconut milk
- Salt and pepper to taste
- 1 onion, chopped
- 4 cups vegetable broth
- 2 tbsp olive oil

Directions:

(1) Olive oil should be heated in a big saucepan over medium heat. (2) Before the onion and garlic become transparent, add them to the pan. (3) Include the vegetable broth and cauliflower. Reduce heat to simmer and cook, covered, for about 20 minutes or until cauliflower is tender. (4) Smooth out the soup by pureeing it with an immersion blender. (5) Add the coconut milk and taste for seasoning. (6) Heat and serve immediately.

BLUEBERRY MACAROONS

Total Time: 25 minutes | Prep Time: 15 minutes

Ingredients:

- 2 cups shredded coconut
- 1/2 cup dried blueberries
- 1/4 cup coconut oil
- 1 cup almond flour
- 1/4 cup honey
- 1/2 tsp vanilla extract

Directions:

(1) Set oven temperature to 350°F, or 175°C. (2) Whisk together almond flour, shredded coconut, honey, coconut oil, and vanilla essence in a bowl. Add dried blueberries and mix well. (3) Blend into a smooth mixture. (4) Divide the batter into small portions and place them on a parchment-lined baking pan. (5) To get a golden brown color, bake for 10 to 12 minutes. (6) Let cool completely before enjoying.

VEGAN GOUDA

Total Time: 15 minutes | Prep Time: 15 minutes

Ingredients:

1/2 cup cashews (soaked for at least 2 hours)	1/2 cup nutritional yeast
1/4 cup coconut oil	1/4 cup tapioca flour
1 tbsp lemon juice	1/2 tsp garlic powder
1/4 tsp smoked paprika	Salt to taste

Directions:

(1) Put the drained cashews into a food processor. (2) Blend in the smoked paprika, nutritional yeast, tapioca flour, coconut oil, lemon juice, garlic powder, and salt. (3) Beat in the cream until completely combined. (4) The consistency should thicken after five to seven minutes of simmering, stirring occasionally, after coming to a boil. (5) Let it cool down before you use it.

NUTELLA COPYCAT SPREAD

Total Time: 15 minutes | Prep Time: 15 minutes

Ingredients:

1 cup hazelnuts, toasted and skinned	1/2 cup cocoa powder
1/4 cup honey or maple syrup	1/4 cup coconut oil
1/4 cup almond milk Pinch of salt	1 tsp vanilla extract

Directions:

(1) To make hazelnut paste, throw the nuts in a food processor and pulse until smooth. (2) Toss in some almond milk, cocoa powder, honey (or maple syrup), salt, coconut oil, and vanilla extract. (3) Blend or process until completely smooth. (4) Pour into a jar and refrigerate until needed.

VANILLA SMOOTHIE

Total Time: 5 minutes | Prep Time: 5 minutes

Ingredients:

1 banana	1 cup almond milk
1/2 cup Greek yogurt	1 tsp vanilla extract
1 tbsp honey or maple syrup (optional)	

Directions:

(1) When using a blender, combine the following Ingredients: banana, almond milk, Greek yogurt, vanilla extract, and either honey or maple syrup. (2) Blend until it is completely smooth. Spoon the concoction into individual glasses and promptly serve.

ALMOND JOY MACAROONS

Total Time: 25 minutes | Prep Time: 15 minutes

Ingredients:

2 cups shredded coconut	1 cup almonds, chopped
1/2 cup dark chocolate chips	1/2 cup almond flour
1/4 cup honey	1/4 cup coconut oil
1/2 tsp vanilla extract	

Directions:

(1) Set oven temperature to 350°F, or 175°C. (2) In the same dish as the shredded coconut, combine the almond flour, flaked almonds, honey, coconut oil, and vanilla extract. Thoroughly mix. (3) Drop the batter by the spoonful onto a parchment-lined baking sheet. (4) To get a golden brown color, bake for 12 to 15 minutes. (5) Drizzle melted dark chocolate chips over the macaroons. (6) Let cool completely before enjoying.

MIXED FRUIT COMPOTE

Total Time: 30 minutes | Prep Time: 10 minutes

Ingredients:

2 cups mixed fresh fruit (e.g., berries, apples, pears)
1 tablespoon lemon juice
1/4 teaspoon ground cinnamon (optional)
1/4 cup honey or maple syrup
1/2 teaspoon vanilla extract

Directions:

(1) Wash the fruit and cut it into little pieces to prepare it. (2) Mix the materials: Put the fruit, honey, lemon juice, vanilla essence, and cinnamon (if desired) into a saucepan and stir to mix. (3) Prepare by reducing the heat to medium and simmering the ingredients. After the fruit has softened and the sauce has thickened slightly, cook for 10 to 15 minutes, stirring regularly. (4) Allow the compote to cool completely before enjoying it. It goes well with yogurt, pancakes, or as a dessert topping and is delicious, both warm and cold.

CHOCOLATE ENERGY BALLS

Total Time: 15 minutes | Prep Time: 10 minutes

Ingredients:

1 cup rolled oats
1/4 cup cocoa powder
1/4 cup chocolate chips (optional)
1/2 cup almond butter
1/4 cup honey or maple syrup
1/4 cup shredded coconut (optional)

Directions:

(1) Combine the almond butter, cocoa powder, honey, and oats in a bowl. Blend into a smooth mixture. (2) Additional Features: If using, stir in chopped coconut and chocolate chips. (3) Create Donuts: Form the mixture into balls no larger than a 1-inch ball. (4) Put in the fridge: Give the balls half an hour to chill in the fridge before you serve them.

CHOCOLATE ALMOND SPREAD

Total Time: 15 minutes | Prep Time: 10 minutes

Ingredients:

1 cup almonds
1/4 cup honey or maple syrup
1/2 teaspoon vanilla extract
1/4 cup cocoa powder
1 tablespoon almond oil or coconut oil
A pinch of salt

Directions:

(1) To process almonds, they should be blended in a food processor until they are absolutely smooth and creamy. This should be done all the way through. (2) Cocoa powder, honey, oil, vanilla extract, and salt are components that should be added to the mixture. Blend until everything is thoroughly combined. (3) In the event that the spread is too thick to obtain the desired consistency, you have the ability to alter the texture by adding a small amount of additional oil to the spread. (4) For storage, place the mixture in a jar and place it in the refrigerator.

VANILLA YOGURT

Total Time: 5 minutes | Prep Time: 5 minutes

Ingredients:

2 cups plain Greek yogurt
2-3 tablespoons honey or maple syrup

1 teaspoon vanilla extract'

Directions:

(1)To combine the ingredients, combine the yogurt, honey, and vanilla essence in a dish and whisk until the mixture is smooth. (2)When ready to eat, serve immediately or chill in the refrigerator until you are ready to consume it.

CHOCOLATE MACAROONS

Total Time: 25 minutes | Prep Time: 10 minutes

Ingredients:

2 cups shredded coconut
1/2 cup honey or maple syrup
1/4 teaspoon salt
1/2 cup cocoa powder
2 large egg whites

Directions:

(1)Put the oven on high heat (350 degrees Fahrenheit, 175 degrees Celsius). (2)In a bowl, combine the shredded coconut, cocoa powder, honey, and salt. Mix until all of the ingredients are equally distributed. (3)To get the egg whites firm, whip them in a separate basin. Add to the coconut mixture while gently folding. (4)Pat the batter into shape by spooning it onto a baking sheet coated with paper. (5)To make the crust golden, bake for 15 to 20 minutes. Chill before you eat.

CHOCOLATE CRINKLE COOKIES

Total Time: 40 minutes | Prep Time: 15 minutes

Ingredients:

1 cup all-purpose flour
1/2 teaspoon baking powder
1/2 cup granulated sugar
1/4 cup melted butter
1/2 teaspoon vanilla extract
1/2 cup cocoa powder
1/4 teaspoon salt
1/4 cup brown sugar
1 large egg
Powdered sugar for rolling

Directions:

(1)Turn the oven on high heat (350°F, 175°C). (2)Flour, cocoa powder, baking soda, and salt are the dry components that need to be mixed in a bowl. (3)Gather Wet Ingredients: In a separate bowl, combine the brown sugar, granulated sugar, melted butter, egg, and vanilla essence. (4)Stir to incorporate after each addition of dry ingredients to wet mixture. (5)Cookie Form: Form dough into balls about an inch in diameter; coat with powdered sugar; set aside to bake. (6)Cook: Cook in the oven for ten to twelve minutes. Let cool completely before enjoying.

WALNUT ENERGY BALLS

Total Time: 15 minutes | Prep Time: 10 minutes

Ingredients:

1 cup walnuts
1/4 cup rolled oats
1/2 teaspoon cinnamon (optional)
1 cup pitted dates
1 tablespoon honey or maple syrup

Directions:

(1)To prepare, pulse the walnuts in a food processor until they are finely chopped. (2)Incorporate Dates: Gradually incorporate the dates into the walnut mixture by blending them thoroughly. (3)Honey, cinnamon (if desired), and rolled oats are the ingredients to be mixed. Mix in the ingredients until they come together. (4)Roll out the mixture and shape it into little balls. (5)Put it in the fridge and let it chill for 30 minutes before serving.

BLACKBERRY ENERGY BALLS

Total Time: 15 minutes | Prep Time: 10 minutes

Ingredients:

1 cup pitted dates

1/2 cup blackberries (fresh or frozen, thawed)

1/2 cup almonds or walnuts

1/4 cup shredded coconut

1 tablespoon chia seeds or flaxseeds

Directions:

(1)To prepare, pulse the walnuts in a food processor until they are finely chopped. (2)Incorporate Dates: Gradually incorporate the dates into the walnut mixture by blending them thoroughly. (3)Honey, cinnamon (if desired), and rolled oats are the ingredients to be mixed. Mix in the ingredients until they come together. (4)Roll out the mixture and shape it into little balls. (5)Put it in the fridge and let it chill for 30 minutes before serving

SESAME SEED ENERGY BALLS

Total Time: 15 minutes | Prep Time: 10 minutes

Ingredients:

1 cup pitted dates

1/2 cup sesame seeds

1/4 cup almond or peanut butter

1/4 cup shredded coconut

1 tablespoon honey or maple syrup

Directions:

(1)The dates should be blended into a paste by being pulsed in a food processor. (2)Blend in the sesame seeds until well-mixed. (3)Mix Other Substitutes: Combine honey, shredded coconut, and almond butter. Mix until thoroughly combined. (4)Crumple into little balls. (5)Allow to chill in the fridge for a minimum of half an hour prior to consumption.

PEANUT BUTTER BANANA SMOOTHIE

Total Time: 5 minutes | Prep Time: 5 minutes

Ingredients:

1 banana, peeled and sliced

2 tablespoons peanut butter

1 cup milk (dairy or non-dairy)

1/2 cup Greek yogurt

1 tablespoon honey (optional)

1/2 teaspoon vanilla extract (optional)

Ice cubes (optional)

Directions:

(1)The dates should be blended into a paste by being pulsed in a food processor. (2)Blend in the sesame seeds until well-mixed. (3)Mix Other Substitutes: Combine honey, shredded coconut, and almond butter. Mix until thoroughly combined. (4)Crumple into little balls. (5)Allow to chill in the fridge for a minimum of half an hour prior to consumption.

SIMPLE PESTO SAUCE

Total Time: 10 minutes | Prep Time: 10 minutes

Ingredients:

2 cups fresh basil leaves

1/2 cup grated Parmesan cheese

1/2 cup pine nuts (or

2 cloves garlic

walnuts)
1/2 cup olive oil   Salt and pepper to taste

Directions:

(1) Put the pine nuts, garlic, Parmesan, basil, and Parmesan into a food processor. (2) Separate the cloves of garlic and mince them. (3) Gradually drizzle olive oil into the pesto while processing until it reaches the desired consistency. (4) Taste and add salt and pepper as needed. (5) Put it to use right away or keep it in the fridge for up to seven days in an airtight container.

MATCHA ENERGY BALLS

Total Time: 15 minutes | Prep Time: 15 minutes

Ingredients:

1 cup pitted dates	1 cup rolled oats
1/4 cup almond butter	2 tablespoons matcha powder
1/4 cup chia seeds	1/4 cup shredded coconut (optional)

Directions:

(1) Run the food processor with the dates and oats added. Chop into fine pieces by blending. (2) Blend in the matcha powder and almond butter. Mix until everything is mixed. (3) Include the chia seeds and mix well. (4) If you'd like, you can roll the mixture into little balls and coat them with shredded coconut. (5) Refrigerate for up to seven days if stored in an airtight container.

CHIPOTLE LIME VINAIGRETTE

Total Time: 5 minutes | Prep Time: 5 minutes

Ingredients:

1/4 cup lime juice   1/4 cup olive oil

1 chipotle pepper in adobo sauce (canned)   1 tablespoon adobo sauce

1 teaspoon honey   1/2 teaspoon ground cumin

Salt to taste

Directions:

1. Combine all ingredients in the food processor. 2. Blend until smooth. 3. Add more salt if necessary to taste. 4. Apply right away or refrigerate for up to seven days if sealed.

PLUM COMPOTE

Total Time: 25 minutes | Prep Time: 10 minutes

Ingredients:

4 cups fresh plums, pitted and chopped	1/2 cup sugar
1/4 cup water	1 teaspoon lemon juice
1/2 teaspoon vanilla extract	

Directions:

(1) In a saucepan, mix together the plums, sugar, and water. (2) For around fifteen to twenty minutes, with the lid on, cook until the plums are soft and the sauce has thickened. (3) After adding the lemon juice and vanilla essence, stir thoroughly. (4) Return to room temperature before slicing. Refrigerate for a maximum of two weeks if stored in an airtight container.

COOKIES WITH CHOCOLATE CHIPS

Total Time: 30 minutes | Prep Times: 15 minutes

Ingredients:

1 cup unsalted butter,   1 cup brown sugar

softened
1/2 cup granulated sugar
2 teaspoons vanilla extract
1 teaspoon baking soda
1/2 teaspoon salt
2 large eggs
3 cups all-purpose flour
1/2 teaspoon baking powder
1 cup chocolate chips

Directions:

Turn the oven on high heat (350°F, 175°C). (2)Whisk together the butter, brown sugar, and granulated sugar in a food processor to make a fluffy mixture. (3)Whisk in the eggs and vanilla essence. Mix everything together. (4)With a whisk, combine the flour, baking soda, baking powder, and salt in a different basin. (5)Slowly add the dry ingredients to the butter mixture and stir until combined. (6)Incorporate the chocolate chips. (7)Spoon dough by the spoonful onto a parchment-lined baking sheet. (8)The edges should be golden brown after 12 to 15 minutes in the oven. (9)After a few minutes of cooling on the baking sheet, move to a wire rack to finish cooling.

BERRY COMPOTE

Total Time: 20 minutes | Prep Time: 10 minutes

Ingredients:

2 cups mixed berries (fresh or frozen)
1/4 cup water
1/4 cup sugar
1 tablespoon lemon juice

Directions:

(1)A saucepan should be used to combine the berries, sugar, and water. (2)Simmer, stirring periodically, for ten to fifteen minutes after the mixture boils or until the berries are tender and the sauce thickens. (3)Add the lemon juice and stir. (4)Prior to serving, allow it to cool down slightly. Place it in an airtight jar and place it in the refrigerator for up to a week.

SPICED FRUIT COMPOTE

Total Time: 30 minutes | Prep Time: 10 minutes

Ingredients

3 cups mixed fruit (apples, pears, peaches), peeled and chopped
1/4 cup water
1/4 teaspoon ground nutmeg
1/2 cup sugar
1 teaspoon ground cinnamon
1/4 teaspoon ground cloves

Directions:

(1)A saucepan should be used to combine the fruit, sugar, and water. (2)Turn the heat down to low and simmer for 20 minutes after the mixture boils or until the fruit is tender and the sauce has thickened. (3)Cinnamon, nutmeg, and cloves should be stirred in. (4)Prior to serving, allow it to cool down slightly. Place it in an airtight jar and place it in the refrigerator for up to a week.

HERB BUTTER

Total Time: 10 minutes | Prep Time: 10 minutes

Ingredients:

1 cup unsalted butter, softened
2 tablespoons fresh chives, chopped
1 garlic clove, minced
2 tablespoons fresh parsley, chopped
1 tablespoon fresh thyme leaves
Salt to taste

Directions:

(1)Put the garlic, butter, parsley, chives, and thyme into the food processor and mix them together. (2)Blend until everything is thoroughly combined. (3)Add salt to taste and season with it. (4)Using a piece of wax paper, shape the mixture into a log and place it in the refrigerator until it becomes hard. You can use it however you choose, for meats, vegetables, or bread.

ITALIAN HERB SPREAD

Total Time: 10 minutes | Prep Time: 10 minutes

Ingredients:

- 1 cup cream cheese, softened
- 2 tablespoons fresh basil, chopped
- 1 tablespoon fresh rosemary, chopped
- Salt and pepper to taste
- 1/2 cup sour cream
- 2 tablespoons fresh oregano, chopped
- 1 garlic clove, minced

Directions:

(1)Combine cream cheese, sour cream, basil, oregano, rosemary, and garlic in the food processor. (2)Blend until smooth. (3)Season with salt and pepper to taste. (4)Use it as a spread on sandwiches or to accompany crackers and bread.

CHOCOLATE HAZELNUT SPREAD

Total Time: 15 minutes | Prep Time: 10 minutes

Ingredients:

- 1 cup roasted hazelnuts
- 1/4 cup unsweetened cocoa powder
- 1/4 cup melted coconut oil
- 1/2 cup powdered sugar
- 1/4 cup milk (or dairy-free milk)
- 1 tsp vanilla extract
- Pinch of salt

Directions:

(1)After roughly 5 minutes of processing, the hazelnuts should be a smooth paste. (2)Salt, cocoa powder, milk, coconut oil, vanilla essence, and powdered sugar should be added. Blend or process until completely smooth. (3)Pour into a jar and refrigerate until needed.

SPICED PUMPKIN SOUP

Total Time: 30 minutes | Prep Time: 10 minutes

Ingredients:

- 1 can (15 oz) pumpkin puree
- 2 cloves garlic, minced
- 1/2 tsp ground cinnamon
- 2 cups vegetable broth
- Salt and pepper to taste
- 1 onion, chopped
- 1 tsp ground cumin
- 1/4 tsp ground nutmeg
- 1 cup coconut milk

Directions:

(1)Chop the garlic and onion finely in a food processor. (2)Put in a big saucepan and cook, stirring occasionally, until tender, about 5 minutes. (3)Crush some cinnamon, nutmeg, and cumin. Add a minute of stirring. (4)Toss in the coconut milk, pumpkin puree, and vegetable broth. After it boils, lower the heat to a simmer and cook for 15 minutes. (5)To make sure the soup is completely smooth, you may either use an immersion blender or carefully return it to the food processor. (6)Try it out, and if necessary, add some salt and pepper. Warm it up before plating.

SWEET AND SOUR SAUCE

Total Time: 10 minutes | Prep Time: 5 minutes

Ingredients:

- 1/2 cup rice vinegar
- 1/4 cup soy sauce
- 2 tbsp cornstarch
- 1/2 cup pineapple juice
- 1/4 cup sugar
- 1/4 cup water

Directions:

(1) Pulse pineapple juice, sugar, soy sauce, and rice vinegar together in a food processor. Incorporate until the sugar has dissolved. (2) The cornstarch and water should be mixed together in a small bowl to produce a slurry. (3) To thicken, transfer the mixture to a saucepan and boil while stirring continuously. (4) Return to room temperature before use.

RICE MILK CHEESE

Total Time: 15 minutes | Prep Time: 10 minutes

Ingredients:

- 1 cup rice milk
- 1/4 cup nutritional yeast
- 1/2 tsp salt
- 1/4 cup tapioca starch
- 1 tbsp lemon juice

Directions:

(1) Run the following ingredients through a food processor: rice milk, tapioca starch, nutritional yeast, salt, and lemon juice. Mix until combined. (2) The mixture should thicken and take on the consistency of cheese when cooked in a pot over medium heat with constant stirring. (3) Immediately place it in a jar for storage and chill until it becomes solid.

ALMOND BUTTER SMOOTHIE

Total Time: 5 minutes | Prep Time: 5 minutes

Ingredients:

- 1 banana
- 1 cup almond milk
- 1/2 tsp vanilla extract
- 1/2 cup almond butter
- 1 tbsp honey or maple syrup
- Ice cubes (optional)

Directions:

(1) Throw in some almond milk, honey (maple syrup or honey), almond butter, banana, and vanilla extract into the food processor. (2) Mix until combined. Toss in some ice cubes and give it another good mix. (3) Serve right away.

PUMPKIN SPICE SPREAD

Total Time: 10 minutes | Prep Time: 10 minutes

Ingredients:

- 1 cup pumpkin puree
- 1/2 tsp ground cinnamon
- 1/4 tsp ground nutmeg
- 1/4 cup maple syrup
- 1/4 tsp ground ginger
- 1/4 tsp ground cloves

Directions:

(1) Mix pumpkin puree, maple syrup, cinnamon, ginger, nutmeg, and cloves in a food processor until smooth. Pour into a jar and refrigerate.

MINT CHOCOLATE SPREAD

Total Time: 15 minutes | Prep Time: 10 minutes

Ingredients:

- 1 cup dark chocolate chips
- 1/4 cup mint extract
- 1/2 cup coconut oil
- 1/4 cup powdered sugar

Directions:

(1)The coconut oil and chocolate chips should be mixed together in a basin that is capable of withstanding the heat of water that is simmering. (2)After everything is melted and smooth, put it in a food processor and mix in the powdered sugar and mint extract. (3)Transfer to an airtight container and chill until solid.

CAULIFLOWER FRITTERS

Total Time: 25 minutes | Prep Time: 15 minutes

Ingredients:

1 head cauliflower, cut into florets
2 eggs
1/4 cup chopped fresh parsley
Olive oil for frying
1/4 cup grated Parmesan cheese
1/2 cup flour
Salt and pepper to taste

Directions:

(1)Get the cauliflower florets soft by steaming them. Give it a little time to cool. (2)Using a food processor, chop the cauliflower into very small pieces. (3)Combine the eggs, flour, Parmesan cheese, parsley, salt, and pepper. Mix everything together. (4)In a skillet set over medium heat, warm the olive oil. Patties should be formed and then cooked in a skillet over medium heat for four minutes on each side or until they have a browned appearance. (5)Place a paper towel over the drained area and serve heat.

CASHEW PARMESAN

Total Time: 10 minutes | Prep Time: 5 minutes

Ingredients:

1 cup raw cashews
1/2 tsp garlic powder
1/4 cup nutritional yeast
1/2 tsp salt

Directions:

(1)Combine cashews in a food processor and process them until they reach a fine crumb consistency. (2)Garlic powder, nutritional yeast, and salt should be added first. Blend until everything is thoroughly combined. (3)Ensure that the container is sealed and place it in the refrigerator.

BRAZILIAN NUT CHEESE

Total Time: 15 minutes | Prep Time: 10 minutes

Ingredients:

1 cup Brazilian nuts
1/4 cup lemon juice
1 garlic clove
1/4 cup nutritional yeast
1/4 cup water
1/2 tsp salt

Directions:

(1)Brazilian nuts should be processed in a food processor until they are completely smooth and form a paste. (2)Salt, nutritional yeast, lemon juice, and water should be added to the mixture. Proceed until the ingredients are completely incorporated. (3)Place in a jar, and then place in the refrigerator.

BABA GANOUSH

Total Time: 30 minutes | Prep Time: 10 minutes

Ingredients:

2 large eggplants
3 tbsp lemon juice
2 tbsp olive oil
Chopped parsley for garnish
1/4 cup tahini
2 cloves garlic, minced
Salt to taste

Directions:

(1) Add some salt, and as a finishing touch, sprinkle some chopped parsley on top. It is recommended to preheat the oven to 400 degrees Fahrenheit (200 degrees Celsius). The eggplants should be pricked with a fork and then roasted on a baking sheet for thirty minutes or until they are soft. **(2)** The flesh should be removed once it has cooled, and then it should be placed in a food processor. **(3)** A mixture of tahini, lemon juice, garlic, and olive oil should be added. Continue to process until smooth.

SUNFLOWER SEED ENERGY BALLS

Total Time: 15 minutes | Prep Time: 10 minutes

Ingredients:

1 cup sunflower seeds
1/4 cup shredded coconut
1/2 tsp vanilla extract
1/2 cup pitted dates
1/4 cup honey

Directions:

(1) To get a finely ground consistency, mix the sunflower seeds in the food processor. **(2)** Incorporate honey, shredded coconut, dates, and vanilla essence into the mixture. It is necessary to process the mixture until it begins to clump together. **(3)** Before refrigerating, roll the mixture into small balls and let it set.

CARAMELIZED ONION DIP

Total Time: 30 minutes | Prep Time: 10 minutes

Ingredients:

2 large onions, thinly sliced
2 tbsp olive oil
1 cup sour cream
1 tbsp balsamic vinegar
1/2 cup mayonnaise
Salt and pepper to taste

Directions:

(1) In a skillet set over medium heat, warm the olive oil. After about 20 minutes of stirring often, add the onions and simmer until they caramelize. **(2)** Let the onions cool down. **(3)** Take the onions that have been caramelized and add them to the food processor along with the sour cream, mayonnaise, balsamic vinegar, salt, and pepper. Combine ingredients and mix until creamy. **(4)** Put in the fridge for a minimum of one hour prior to consumption.

ROASTED RED PEPPER DIP

Total Time: 20 minutes | Prep Time: 10 minutes

Ingredients:

2 roasted red peppers (jarred or homemade)
1/4 cup tahini
2 tbsp lemon juice
1 garlic clove
Salt to taste

Directions:

(1) Blend together garlic, tahini, lemon juice, and roasted red peppers in a food processor. **(2)** Whip till completely smooth. Taste and add salt as desired. **(3)** Paredes with pita chips.

CARROT GINGER SOUP

Total Time: 40 minutes | Prep Time: 10 minutes

Ingredients:

1 tbsp olive oil
4 cups carrots, peeled
1 onion, chopped
2 tbsp fresh ginger,

and chopped
4 cups vegetable broth
Salt and pepper to taste
minced
1 cup coconut milk

Directions:

(1)Olive oil should be heated in a big saucepan over medium heat. Prepare the onion by sautéing it for about five minutes or until it reaches the desired tenderness. (2)After the ginger and carrots have been added, continue to cook for an additional five minutes. (3)When the saucepan has reached a boil, add the vegetable broth to it and stir it around. After 20 minutes of simmering, the carrots should be soft. (4)Use a blender or food processor to purée the soup until it is absolutely smooth. This should take about a minute. Get back into the pot. (5)Add the coconut milk just before serving, and add salt and pepper before heating.

CINNAMON ROLL ENERGY BALLS

Total Time: 15 minutes | Prep Time: 15 minutes

Ingredients:

1 cup pitted dates
1 tsp ground cinnamon
1/4 cup almond flour
1 cup raw cashews
1/4 tsp ground nutmeg
1/4 cup shredded coconut (optional)

Directions:

(1)In a food processor, mix together the cashews and dates. The mixture will begin to come together after processing until finely chopped. (2)Incorporate the almond flour, cinnamon, and nutmeg. Whip until combined. (3)If you'd like, roll the mixture into little balls and sprinkle some shredded coconut on top. (4)The food should be allowed to chill in the refrigerator for half an hour before being consumed.

LEMON MACAROONS

Total Time: 30 minutes | Prep Time: 15 minutes

Ingredients:

2 cups shredded unsweetened coconut
1/2 cup honey
1 tsp lemon zest
1/2 cup almond flour
1/4 cup lemon juice

Directions:

(1)Adjust the temperature of the oven to 325 degrees Fahrenheit (163 degrees Celsius). Put parchment paper on a baking pan. (2)Honey, almond flour, coconut, lemon zest, and juice should all be mixed together in a food processor. Blend until combined. (3)Spoon the batter onto the preheated baking sheet. (4)To get golden brown edges, bake for about 15 minutes. (5)Chill before you eat.

COOKIE DOUGH ENERGY BALLS

Total Time: 15 minutes | Prep Time: 15 minutes

Ingredients:

1 cup pitted dates
1/4 cup almond flour
1 tsp vanilla extract
1 cup raw cashews
1/4 cup mini chocolate chips

Directions:

(1)In a food processor, mix together the cashews and dates. The mixture will begin to come together after processing until finely chopped. (2)Combine the vanilla extract and almond flour. Whip until combined. (3)Incorporate the chocolate chips. (4)Form tiny balls from the mixture. (5)Put in the fridge for a minimum of half an hour prior to consumption.

WHITE CHOCOLATE SPREAD

Total Time: 10 minutes | Prep Time: 10 minutes

Ingredients:

1 cup white chocolate chips	1/2 cup cashew butter
1/4 cup coconut oil	1 tsp vanilla extract

Directions:

(1)Use a double boiler or a bowl that can be microwaved to melt the white chocolate chips and coconut oil. (2)In a food processor, combine melted chocolate, cashew butter, and vanilla extract. Process until smooth. (3)Transfer to a jar and let cool. Store in the refrigerator.

POTATO PANCAKES

Total Time: 30 minutes | Prep Time: 15 minutes

Ingredients:

4 large potatoes, peeled and grated	1 onion, grated
2 eggs	1/4 cup flour
Salt and pepper to taste	Oil for frying

Directions:

(1)The grated potatoes and onion should be mixed together in a big basin. Ensure that all surplus moisture is squeezed out. (2)Flour, eggs, salt, and pepper should be added. Be sure to mix thoroughly. (3)Grease a skillet and set it over medium heat. (4)Flatten spoonfuls of the mixture with a spatula after dropping them onto the skillet. About three to four minutes per side, cook until golden brown. (5)Before serving, drain well using paper towels.

RICE MILK YOGURT

Total Time: 24 hours | Prep Time: 10 minutes

Ingredients:

4 cups rice milk

1/4 cup plain yogurt (store-bought or homemade)

Directions:

(1)Bring rice milk to a boil in a saucepan and cook until it reaches 110°F, or 43°C. (2)Fill a separate bowl or jar with the rice milk. (3)Blend in nonfat yogurt. (4)After the first 12 to 24 hours of covering with a cloth, set aside in a warm location. (5)Chill before consuming.

THAI PEANUT SAUCE

Total Time: 10 minutes | Prep Time: 10 minutes

Ingredients:

1/2 cup peanut butter	1/4 cup soy sauce
2 tbsp honey	1 tbsp rice vinegar
1 garlic clove, minced	1 tsp grated ginger
Water as needed	

Directions:

(1)Put peanut butter, ginger, rice vinegar, soy sauce, honey, and garlic into a food processor. Whip till completely smooth. (2)To get the consistency you want, add water little by little. (3)Feel free to serve it right away or keep it in the fridge for later..

GARLIC BUTTER

Total Time: 10 minutes | Prep Time: 10 minutes

Ingredients:

1/2 cup unsalted butter,   4 garlic cloves, minced

softened
2 tbsp fresh parsley, chopped
Salt to taste

Directions:

(1) Put the garlic, parsley, salt, butter, and a bowl or food processor to work together. (2) Beat until everything is blended. (3) Keep refrigerated or use right away.

ALMOND CHOCOLATE SPREAD

Total Time: 10 minutes | Prep Time: 10 minutes

Ingredients:

1 cup almonds
1 tbsp honey
1/2 cup dark chocolate chips
1/4 tsp vanilla extract

Directions:

(1) Roast for 10 minutes at 350°F (175°C), then take off the heat and let cool. (2) Smoothly puree the almonds in a food processor. (3) Combine almond butter, honey, vanilla essence, and melted dark chocolate chips. (4) Mix until everything is mixed. (5) Put it in a jar and put it in the fridge.

PISTACHIO BUTTER

Total Time: 10 minutes | Prep Time: 10 minutes

Ingredients:

2 cups shelled pistachios
1 tbsp coconut oil (optional)
1 tbsp honey (optional)

Directions:

(1) Blend the pistachios in a food processor until they are completely smooth, stopping to scrape down the sides as necessary. (2) After you've blended everything together, feel free to add honey and coconut oil if you like. (3) Place the mixture in a jar, and then put it in the refrigerator..

CASHEW MILK YOGURT

Total Time: 24 hours | Prep Time: 10 minutes

Ingredients:

2 cups cashews, soaked overnight
1/4 cup plain yogurt (store-bought or homemade)
4 cups water

Directions:

(1) Wash and drain cashews that have been soaked. (2) Add the cashews and water to a blender and pulse until smooth. The mixture should be smooth. (3) It should be transferred to a clean bowl or jar. (4) Stir in plain yogurt. (5) After the first 12 to 24 hours of covering with a cloth, set aside in a warm location. (6) Refrigerate before serving.

FRENCH ONION DIP

Total Time: 20 minutes | Prep Time: 10 minutes

Ingredients:

1 cup sour cream
1/2 cup finely chopped onion
1/2 tsp salt
1/2 cup mayonnaise
1 tsp garlic powder

Directions:

(1) Sour cream, mayonnaise, chopped onion, garlic powder, and salt should be mixed together in a bowl by the individual. **(2)** After thoroughly combining, mix. **(3)** Before serving, place in the refrigerator for at least one hour.

MUSHROOM SOUP

Total Time: 40 minutes | Prep Time: 10 minutes

Ingredients:

- 1 tbsp olive oil
- 4 cups mushrooms, sliced
- 1 cup heavy cream
- 1 onion, chopped
- 4 cups vegetable broth
- Salt and pepper to taste

Directions:

(1) Olive oil should be heated in a big saucepan over medium heat. Cook the onion until it softens, which should take around 5 minutes. **(2)** After about 10 minutes of cooking, add the mushrooms and let them release their juices. **(3)** Before adding the veggie broth, bring it to a boil. Bring to a simmer and cover for 15 minutes. **(4)** Puree or blend the soup until it reaches a velvety smooth consistency. Get back into the pot. **(5)** Once the heavy cream has been stirred in, add the salt and pepper. Once heated, proceed to serve.

MAPLE PECAN SPREAD

Total Time: 10 minutes | Prep Time: 10 minutes

Ingredients:

- 1 cup pecans
- 1/4 cup pure maple syrup
- 1/4 cup coconut oil
- 1/2 teaspoon vanilla extract

Directions:

(2) After approximately 5 minutes of toasting in a dry skillet over medium heat, the pecans should smell nutty. When cooled, remove from heat. **(3)** To make pecan powder, pulse nuts in a food processor until they are finely ground. **(4)** Season with salt, vanilla extract, coconut oil, maple syrup, and coconut oil. Beat in the cream until completely combined. **(5)** Put it in the fridge in a sealed jar.

CASHEW ENERGY BALLS

Total Time: 15 minutes | Prep Time: 15 minutes

Ingredients:

- 1 cup cashews
- 1/4 cup shredded coconut
- 1/4 teaspoon vanilla extract
- 1 cup pitted dates
- 1 tablespoon chia seeds

Directions:

(1) In a food processor, grind the cashews until they are finely ground. **(2)** Complement with chia seeds, shredded coconut, dates, and vanilla extract. Mix until a ball forms when you press down on the mixture. **(3)** Pat the mixture into balls about 1 inch in diameter. **(4)** Put it in the fridge in a sealed jar.

HEMP MILK YOGURT

Total Time: 12 hours (including fermentation) | Prep Time: 15 minutes

Ingredients:

2 cups hemp milk

1/4 cup plain vegan yogurt (as a starter culture)

1 tablespoon agar-agar powder

Directions:

(1) Turn off the heat and let the hemp milk cool to around 110 degrees Fahrenheit after heating it to 180 degrees. (2) Add the agar-agar powder and vegan yogurt and mix well. (3) Transfer the mixture to a sterilized, tightly sealed jar, seal it, and set it aside to steep for 8 to 12 hours in a warm location, such as a warmed oven. (4) Chill before consuming.

ROASTED RED PEPPER SAUCE

Total Time: 30 minutes | Prep Time: 10 minutes

Ingredients:

4 large red bell peppers

2 cloves garlic

1/4 cup olive oil

1 tablespoon balsamic vinegar

Salt and pepper to taste

Directions:

(1) While rotating once or twice, blacken the skins of the bell peppers by roasting them under a broiler. Cover with plastic wrap and place in a separate location to steam. (2) Extract the seeds by peeling off the skins. Bring the garlic and roasted peppers together in a food processor. (3) A few drops of balsamic vinegar should be sprinkled over the topping in addition to the salt and pepper. Whip till completely smooth. (4) Put it in the fridge in a sealed jar..

ARTICHOKE DIP

Total Time: 10 minutes | Prep Time: 10 minutes

Ingredients:

1 can artichoke hearts, drained

1 cup Greek yogurt

1/2 cup grated Parmesan cheese

2 cloves garlic

Salt and pepper to taste

Directions:

(1) It is recommended that a food processor be used to combine artichoke hearts, Greek yogurt, Parmesan cheese, and garlic. (2) Until the mixture is silky smooth and creamy. (3) In addition to seasoning with salt, add pepper and salt to taste. (4) It can be served either chilled or at room temperature.

MACADAMIA NUT COOKIES

Total Time: 30 minutes | Prep Time: 15 minutes

Ingredients:

1 cup macadamia nuts

1/2 cup coconut flour

1/4 cup honey

1/4 cup coconut oil

1/2 teaspoon vanilla extract

Pinch of salt

Directions:

(1) Set oven temperature to 350°F, or 175°C. (2) Pulse them in a food processor to make finely chopped macadamia nuts. (3) Combine the vanilla extract, salt, honey, coconut oil, and flour made from coconuts. Mix until a dough is formed. (4) On a baking sheet, flatten the dough slightly after rolling it into little balls. (5) To get a golden brown color, bake for 10 to 12 minutes.

GINGER ENERGY BALLS

Total Time: 15 minutes | Prep Time: 15 minutes

Ingredients:

- 1 cup almonds
- 1 tablespoon fresh ginger, grated
- 1 cup pitted dates
- 1/4 cup chia seeds

Directions:

(1) Pulse the almonds in a food processor until they reach a fine, powdery consistency. (2) Dates, ginger, and chia seeds should be added. The mixture should be processed until it becomes cohesive. (3) Form the mixture into balls about one inch in diameter. (4) Ensure that the container is sealed and place it in the refrigerator.

APPLE CINNAMON SPREAD

Total Time: 20 minutes | Prep Time: 10 minutes

Ingredients:

- 2 large apples, peeled and chopped
- 1 teaspoon cinnamon
- 1/4 cup honey
- 1 tablespoon lemon juice

Directions:

(1) Chop the apples into a smooth puree in a food processor. (2) Place in a pot and proceed to incorporate honey, cinnamon, and lemon juice. (3) Ten minutes of stirring occasionally over medium heat should be enough to thicken the mixture. (4) After letting cool, transfer to a sealed container and refrigerate.

HEMP SEED ENERGY BALLS

Total Time: 15 minutes | Prep Time: 15 minutes

Ingredients:

- 1 cup hemp seeds
- 1/4 cup coconut flakes
- 1 cup pitted dates
- 1 tablespoon chia seeds

Directions:

(1) Grind the hemp seeds to a fine powder in a food processor. (2) Incorporate chia seeds, coconut flakes, and dates. Combine all ingredients and process until a dough forms. (3) Pat the mixture into balls about 1 inch in diameter. (4) Put it in the fridge in a sealed jar.

SWEET POTATO SOUP

Total Time: 45 minutes | Prep Time: 15 minutes

Ingredients:

- 2 large sweet potatoes, peeled and chopped
- 2 cloves garlic, minced
- 1 tablespoon olive oil
- 1 onion, chopped
- 4 cups vegetable broth
- Salt and pepper to taste

Directions:

(1) Over medium heat, gently reheat the olive oil in a large saucepan. Sauté the garlic and onion until they become transparent. (2) Then, throw in some sweet potatoes and veggie stock. Simmer for approximately 25 minutes, or until sweet potatoes are soft, after bringing to a boil. (3) Smoothly purée the soup in a food processor or immersion blender. (4) To taste, season with salt and pepper, depending on your preferences. Hot is best.

PEAR COMPOTE

Total Time: 30 minutes | Prep Time: 10 minutes

Ingredients:

- 4 ripe pears, peeled and chopped
- 1/4 cup honey

1 teaspoon cinnamon   1 tablespoon lemon juice

Directions:

(1) Put the lemon juice, cinnamon, honey, and pears in a pot. (2) Ten minutes to twenty minutes over medium heat is approximately right for softening the pears and thickening the mixture. (3) Chill before you eat.

LENTIL SOUP

Total Time: 45 minutes | Prep Time: 15 minutes

Ingredients:

1 cup dried lentils   1 onion, chopped
2 carrots, chopped   2 celery stalks, chopped
4 cups vegetable broth   2 cloves garlic, minced
1 teaspoon cumin   Salt and pepper to taste

Directions:

(1) After rinsing with cold water, leave lentils aside. (2) Prepare the olive oil by heating it in a large saucepan over a medium flame. Sauté the garlic, onion, carrots, celery, and garlic until they are soft. (3) Spice up the lentils with cumin, vegetable broth, salt, and pepper. Bring to a boil, then reduce heat to low and simmer for thirty minutes or until lentils are tender. (4) For a creamier texture, you can puree some of the soup in a food processor or immersion blender if you like.

VEGETABLE SOUP BASE

Total Time: 1 hour | Prep Time: 15 minutes

Ingredients:

2 cups mixed vegetables   4 cups vegetable broth
(carrots, celery, onions)
2 cloves garlic, minced   1 bay leaf
Salt and pepper to taste

Directions:

(1) Olive oil should be heated in a big saucepan over medium heat. Sauté the garlic and a mixture of vegetables until they soften. (2) Bay leaf and vegetable broth should be added. Simmer for half an hour after bringing to a boil. (3) Try it out, and if necessary, add some salt and pepper. This can be used as a base for stews or soups.

+POTATO LEEK SOUP

Total Time: 45 minutes | Prep Time: 15 minutes

Ingredients:

4 large potatoes, peeled   2 leeks, cleaned and
and chopped   chopped
4 cups vegetable broth   2 cloves garlic, minced
2 tablespoons olive oil   Salt and pepper to taste

Directions:

(1) In a big saucepan, warm the olive oil over medium heat. Saute the garlic and leeks until they soften. (2) Make a broth with potatoes and vegetables. After the mixture boils, lower the heat and simmer for approximately 25 minutes or until the potatoes are soft. (3) Smoothly purée the soup in a food processor or immersion blender. (4) For flavor, add salt and

ALMOND JOY ENERGY BALLS

Total Time: 15 minutes | Prep Time: 15 minutes

Ingredients:

1 cup almonds   1 cup pitted dates

1/4 cup cocoa powder

1/4 cup mini chocolate chips (optional)

Pinch of salt

1/4 cup shredded coconut

1/2 teaspoon vanilla extract

Directions:

(1) Pulse the almonds in a food processor until they are finely crushed. (2) If used, stir in the chocolate chips, shredded coconut, dates, cocoa powder, salt, and vanilla essence. (3) Mix everything together until it becomes sticky. (4) Once you have formed the dough into balls with a diameter of approximately one inch, place them on a baking sheet. (5) Chill for half an hour before serving..

CREAMED SPINACH

Total Time: 25 minutes | Prep Time: 10 minutes

Ingredients:

1 pound fresh spinach

1 onion, finely chopped

1 cup heavy cream

Salt and pepper to taste

2 tablespoons olive oil

2 cloves garlic, minced

1/4 teaspoon nutmeg

Directions:

(1) In a big pot of hot water, cook the spinach for two to three minutes, until it softens. Remove extra water by draining and pressing. (2) Mince the spinach by pulsing it in a food processor. (3) Put the olive oil in a skillet and place it over medium heat. Stir in the garlic and onion, cooking until the vegetables are soft. (4) Chop some spinach and toss it in a pan. Saute it for around 5 minutes. (5) Combine the nutmeg and thick cream. In about 5 minutes, the cream should have thickened. (6) Add pepper and salt to taste..

MAPLE BUTTER

Total Time: 10 minutes | Prep Time: 10 minutes

Ingredients:

1 cup unsalted butter, softened

1/2 teaspoon vanilla extract

1/4 cup pure maple syrup

Directions:

(1) Put the melted butter, maple syrup, and vanilla extract in a food processor and blend them together. (2) Mix until it's creamy and smooth. (3) Put it in a jar and put it in the fridge until you're ready to use it.

OLIVE TAPENADE

Total Time: 10 minutes | Prep Time: 10 minutes

Ingredients:

1 cup pitted Kalamata olives

1/4 cup capers

2 tablespoons olive oil

1 tablespoon fresh parsley, chopped

1/2 cup pitted green olives

2 cloves garlic

1 tablespoon lemon juice

Directions:

(1) Combine the garlic, olives, and capers in a food processor and process until smooth. Pulse until extremely finely minced. (2) After adding the lemon juice and olive oil, continue processing until everything is thoroughly blended. (3) Toss with the chopped fresh parsley. (4) Immediately serve or store in the refrigerator for later use.

VEGAN MAYONNAISE

Total Time: 5 minutes | Prep Time: 5 minutes

Ingredients:

- 1/2 cup unsweetened soy milk
- 1 tablespoon apple cider vinegar
- 1 teaspoon Dijon mustard
- 1/2 cup neutral oil
- 1 tablespoon lemon juice
- 1/2 teaspoon salt

Directions:

(1) The soy milk, apple cider vinegar, lemon juice, Dijon mustard, and salt should be mixed together in a food processor. (2) While the machine is operating, slowly add the oil to the mixture. Do this again and again until the mixture thickens and emulsifies. (3) Refrigerate for up to a week after it has been prepared.

QUICK SALSA

Total Time: 10 minutes | Prep Time: 10 minutes

Ingredients:

- 4 medium tomatoes, chopped
- 1 jalapeño, seeded and chopped
- 2 tablespoons fresh cilantro, chopped
- Salt to taste
- 1/2 onion, finely chopped
- 2 cloves garlic, minced
- Juice of 1 lime

Directions:

(1) Put the tomatoes, onion, jalapeño, garlic, cilantro, and lime juice into a food combine all of the ingredients in the processor. (2) Combine all of the ingredients and pulse until the mixture achieves the desired consistency. (3) Season with salt and add more if needed. (4) If you want to serve it cold, chill it first.

CINNAMON MACAROONS

Total Time: 25 minutes | Prep Time: 15 minutes

Ingredients:

- 2 cups shredded coconut
- 1/2 cup maple syrup
- 1/4 teaspoon salt
- 1 cup almond flour
- 1 teaspoon ground cinnamon
- 2 large egg whites

Directions:

(1) Heating the oven to 175 degrees Celsius (350 degrees Fahrenheit) is the recommended temperature. Before you begin, line a baking pan with parchment paper. (2) Put all of the ingredients (shredded coconut, almond flour, maple syrup, cinnamon, salt) into a food processor and blend until smooth. (3) Blend in the egg whites until they are thoroughly combined. (4) Spoonfuls of the mixture should be dropped onto the prepared baking sheet. For fifteen to twenty minutes, or until the top is golden brown. Prior to serving, allow it to cool totally.

SPINACH SPREAD

Total Time: 10 minutes | Prep Time: 10 minutes

Ingredients:

- 2 cups fresh spinach
- 1/4 cup fresh basil leaves
- 1 tablespoon lemon juice
- 1/2 cup Greek yogurt
- 2 cloves garlic
- Salt and pepper to taste

Directions:

(1) In a food processor, blend the spinach, Greek yogurt, basil, garlic, and lemon juice until the ingredients are well incorporated. (2) Maintain a

smooth consistency. (3)Use pepper and salt to season the food. (4)Before serving, chill the food.

VANILLA MACAROONS

Total Time: 25 minutes | Prep Time: 15 minutes

Ingredients:

2 cups shredded coconut	1 cup almond flour
1/2 cup maple syrup	1 teaspoon vanilla extract
1/4 teaspoon salt	2 large egg whites

Directions:

(1)Process the spinach, Greek yogurt, basil, and garlic; mix the juice of one lemon together in a food processor until everything is thoroughly blended. (2)Maintain a smooth consistency. (3)Use pepper and salt to season the food. (4)Before serving, chill the food. (5)Bake for 15-20 minutes, or until golden brown. (6)Cool completely before serving

SWEET VEGAN CHEESE

Total Time: 10 minutes | Prep Time: 10 minutes

Ingredients:

1 cup raw cashews	1/4 cup nutritional yeast
1 tablespoon lemon juice	1 tablespoon maple syrup
1/4 teaspoon turmeric (for color)	Salt to taste

Directions:

(1)The soaked cashews should be drained and rinsed. The cashews, nutritional yeast, salt, maple syrup, turmeric, and lemon juice should all be mixed together in a food processor. (2)Process until smooth and creamy. Make any required adjustments to the seasoning, then place in the refrigerator until ready to use.

COMPOUND BUTTER

Total Time: 10 minutes | Prep Time: 10 minutes

Ingredients:

1 cup unsalted butter, softened	2 tablespoons fresh herbs (such as parsley, chives
1 clove garlic, minced Salt and pepper to taste	1 tablespoon lemon zest

Directions:

(1)Butter that has been softened, fresh herbs, garlic, and the zest of a lemon should be combined in a food processor. (2)Continue processing until everything is thoroughly blended. (3)Use pepper and salt to season the food. (4)Place in a container and chill in the refrigerator until it becomes solid.

DATE SPREAD

Total Time: 10 minutes | Prep Time: 10 minutes

Ingredients:

1 cup pitted dates	1/4 cup water
1/4 cup chopped nuts (optional)	1/2 teaspoon vanilla extract

Directions:

(1)Dates and water should be mixed together in a food processor. (2)Maintain a smooth consistency. (3)The vanilla extract and chopped nuts should be stirred in. (4)Put it in a jar and put it in the refrigerator.

PIMENTO CHEESE

Total Time: 10 minutes | Prep Time: 10 minutes

Ingredients:

1 cup shredded sharp cheddar cheese	1/2 cup mayonnaise
1/4 cup pimentos, chopped	1/4 teaspoon garlic powder
1/4 teaspoon onion powder	Salt and pepper to taste

Directions:

(1)Cheese, mayonnaise, picante peppers, garlic powder, and onion powder should be mixed together in a food processor. (2)Make sure everything is thoroughly blended. (3)Salt and pepper should be used to season. (4)Before serving, you should chill.

PECAN ENERGY BALLS

Total Time: 15 minutes | Prep Time: 15 minutes

Ingredients:

1 cup pecans	1 cup pitted dates
1/4 cup shredded coconut	1/4 cup cacao nibs (optional)
1/2 teaspoon vanilla extract	Pinch of salt

Directions:

(1)In a food processor, pulse the pecans until finely ground. (2)Add the dates, shredded coconut, cacao nibs (if using), vanilla extract, and salt. (3)Process until the mixture is well combined and sticky. (4)Form the dough into balls measuring one inch in diameter and move them to a baking sheet. (5)Refrigerate for at least 30 minutes before serving.

CINNAMON SUGAR SPREAD

Total Time: 10 minutes | Prep Time: 10 minutes

Ingredients:

1 cup unsalted butter, softened	1/2 cup brown sugar
1/4 cup granulated sugar	1 tablespoon ground cinnamon
1/2 teaspoon vanilla extract	

Directions:

(1)In a food processor, combine softened butter, brown sugar, granulated sugar, cinnamon, and vanilla extract. Perform a series of pulses on the mixture until it is entirely smooth. (2)Mix until it is completely smooth and properly blended. (3)Before using, place the mixture in a jar and place it in the refrigerator for at least an hour.

BLACK BEAN BURGERS

Total Time: 30 minutes | Prep Time: 10 minutes

Ingredients:

1 can (15 oz) black beans, drained and rinsed	1/2 cup breadcrumbs
1/2 cup finely chopped onion	1/2 cup grated carrot
1/4 cup chopped fresh cilantro	1 egg
1 tablespoon chili powder	1 teaspoon cumin
Salt and pepper to taste	

Directions:

(1) Using a food processor, the black beans should be pulsed until they are almost completely mashed but still retain some sort of chunkiness. **(2)** Incorporate the breadcrumbs, carrot, onion, cilantro, egg, cumin, chili powder, salt, and pepper. Blend everything together until smooth. **(3)** Shape into patties the mixture. **(4)** Cook the patties in a skillet over medium heat for four to five minutes on each side or until they are cooked through and have a golden brown color.

COCONUT ALMOND ENERGY BALLS

Total Time: 15 minutes | Prep Time: 15 minutes

Ingredients:

1 cup almonds
1/2 cup pitted dates
1/2 teaspoon vanilla extract
1 cup shredded coconut
2 tablespoons coconut oil

Directions:

(1) Pulse the almonds and shredded coconut together in a food processor until they are finely pulverized. **(2)** Incorporate the dates, coconut oil, and vanilla essence. Mix until the ingredients clump together. **(3)** Before serving, chill the mixture for at least 30 minutes after rolling it into little balls.

CHIA SEED CHEESE

Total Time: 10 minutes | Prep Time: 10 minutes

Ingredients:

1 cup cashews, soaked for 2 hours
1/4 cup water
2 tablespoons chia seeds
1 tablespoon lemon juice
1 tablespoon nutritional yeast
Salt to taste

Directions:

(1) Soaked cashews should be drained and rinsed. Place in a food processor along with water, nutritional yeast, chia seeds, lemon juice, and salt. Process until smooth. **(2)** Until the mixture is silky smooth and creamy. **(3)** Before serving, place the mixture in a jar and place it in the refrigerator for at least an hour.

ALMOND MILK YOGURT

Total Time: 10 minutes | Prep Time: 10 minutes

Ingredients:

4 cups almond milk (unsweetened)
1 tablespoon sweetener (optional)
1/4 cup almond yogurt starter or probiotic powder

Directions:

(1) In a saucepan, bring the temperature of the almond milk to 110 degrees Fahrenheit (43 degrees Celsius). **(2)** Incorporate the probiotic powder or yogurt starter into the mixture. **(3)** Once the mixture has been transferred to a clean jar or container, cover it and allow it to remain in a warm place for six to eight hours or overnight. **(4)** Put the mixture in the refrigerator after it has thickened.

PECAN SANDIES

Total Time: 25 minutes | Prep Time: 10 minutes

Ingredients:

Ingredients:

1 cup pecans
1/2 cup butter, softened
1/4 teaspoon salt
1 cup all-purpose flour
1/2 cup granulated sugar
1/2 teaspoon vanilla extract

Directions:

(1) Bake for 12–15 minutes, or until the edges turn golden, after preheating the oven to 350°F (175°C). In a food processor, grind the pecans until they are finely ground. In a bowl, cream the butter, sugar, and vanilla extract until fluffy. Gradually mix in the flour, ground pecans, and salt. First, roll the dough into small balls, and then slightly flatten each ball.

HONEY WALNUT SPREAD

Total Time: 15 minutes | Prep Time: 15 minutes

Ingredients:

1 cup walnuts
1 tablespoon coconut oil
1/4 cup honey
1/2 teaspoon cinnamon

Directions:

(1) Process the walnuts in a food processor until they reach a creamy consistency. (2) Combine cinnamon, honey, and coconut oil. Combine all ingredients by blending. (3) Place in an airtight jar and chill.

NUT AND SEED GRANOLA

Total Time: 40 minutes | Prep Time: 10 minutes

Ingredients:

2 cups rolled oats
1/2 cup pumpkin seeds
1/2 cup almonds, chopped
1/4 cup sunflower seeds
1/4 cup honey or maple syrup
1/2 teaspoon cinnamon
1/4 cup coconut oil
Salt to taste

Directions:

(1) Set oven temperature to 350°F, or 175°C. (2) Combine the oats, almonds, sunflower seeds, and pumpkin seeds in a big basin. (3) Honey (or maple syrup) and coconut oil should be melted together in a small pot over low heat. (4) Toss the oat mixture with the honey mixture and mix until evenly coated. (5) Evenly distribute the mixture onto a baking sheet and bake, stirring once halfway through, for 30 minutes. (6) Let it cool entirely before putting it away.

SUNFLOWER SEED CHEESE

Total Time: 10 minutes | Prep Time: 10 minutes

Ingredients:

2 tablespoons nutritional yeast
Salt to taste
1/4 cup water
1 tablespoon lemon juice

Directions:

(1) Soaked sunflower seeds should be drained and rinsed. In a food processor, combine the ingredients, including water, nutritional yeast, lemon juice, and salt. (2) Until the mixture is silky smooth and creamy. (3) Before serving, place the mixture in a jar and place it in the refrigerator for at least one hour..

OLIVE SPREAD

Total Time: 15 minutes | Prep Time: 15 minutes

Ingredients:

1 cup pitted olives (black or green)	1/4 cup olive oil
1 tablespoon lemon juice	1 garlic clove
1 tablespoon capers (optional)	

Directions:

(1) Add the olives, olive oil, lemon juice, garlic, and capers (if you are using them) to a food processor and pulse until smooth. (2) Using additional olive oil as required, process until the mixture is completely smooth. (3) After transferring to a container, place in the refrigerator until ready to serve.

VEGAN CHEDDAR

Total Time: 20 minutes | Prep Time: 10 minutes

Ingredients:

1 cup cashews, soaked for 2 hours	1/2 cup nutritional yeast
1/4 cup lemon juice	1/4 cup water
1 tablespoon turmeric	1 teaspoon smoked paprika
Salt to taste	

Directions:

(1) Soaked cashews should be drained and rinsed. Combine the nutritional yeast, lemon juice, water, turmeric, paprika, and salt in a food processor. Place the mixture in the food processor until the mixture is silky, smooth, and creamy. (2) Moving the mixture to a container, chill it in the refrigerator before serving.

BLACK BEAN DIP

Total Time: 10 minutes | Prep Time: 10 minutes

Ingredients:

1 can (15 oz) black beans,	1/4 cup lime juice
1/4 cup fresh cilantro	1/4 cup olive oil
1 garlic clove	1/2 teaspoon cumin
Salt and pepper to taste	

Directions:

(1) Put the black beans, lime juice, cilantro, olive oil, garlic, and cumin into a food processor and process until fully combined. (2) Maintain a smooth consistency. (3) Salt and pepper should be used to taste, and salt should be used to season. It can be served either chilled or at room temperature.

MEDITERRANEAN SPREAD

Total Time: 15 minutes | Prep Time: 15 minutes

Ingredients:

1 cup cooked chickpeas	1/4 cup sun-dried tomatoes
1/4 cup olives	2 tablespoons olive oil
1 tablespoon lemon juice	1 garlic clove
1/2 teaspoon dried oregano	Salt and pepper to taste

Directions:

(1) Put the chickpeas, sun-dried tomatoes, olives, olive oil, lemon juice, garlic, and oregano into a food processor and pulse until everything is combined. (2) Maintain a smooth consistency. (3) Add salt and pepper to taste, and season with salt. It is possible to serve it either hot or cold, depending on your preference.

COFFEE ENERGY BALLS

Total Time: 15 minutes | Prep Time: 15 minutes

Ingredients:

1 cup pitted dates

1/2 cup nuts (e.g., almonds, cashews)

2 tablespoons coffee grounds

1 tablespoon cocoa powder

1 tablespoon coconut oil

Directions:

(1)Dates, almonds, coffee grounds, cocoa powder, and coconut oil should be mixed together in a food processor until the mixture remains cohesive. (2)Then, the mixture should be rolled into small balls and placed in the refrigerator for at least half an hour before being served.

APPLE CINNAMON ENERGY BALLS

Total Time: 15 minutes | Prep Time: 15 minutes

Ingredients:

1 cup rolled oats

1/2 cup dried apples, chopped

1/4 cup ground almonds

1/4 cup honey or maple syrup

1 tsp ground cinnamon

1/4 cup almond butter

1/4 cup shredded coconut (optional)

Directions:

(1)Combine the oats, dried apples, ground almonds, and cinnamon in a food processor. Process until fully combined. Combine thoroughly by pulsing. (2)Put in the almond butter and honey (or maple syrup, if you want). Perform a series of pulses until the mixture begins to bind together. (3)The mixture should be rolled into little balls with a diameter of approximately one inch. You can choose to roll the balls with shredded coconut if you wish. (4)You may keep it in the refrigerator for up to two weeks if you store it in an airtight container.

SUN-DRIED TOMATO DIP

Total Time: 10 minutes | Prep Time: 10 minutes

Ingredients:

1 cup sun-dried tomatoes (preferably in oil)

1/2 cup walnuts

1/4 cup fresh basil leaves

2 cloves garlic

1/4 cup olive oil

Salt and pepper to taste

Directions:

(1)Sun-dried tomatoes, walnuts, basil, and garlic should be mixed together in a food processor. Pulse until the mixture is coarsely minced. (2)To achieve the proper consistency of the dip, gradually include the olive oil while the processor is operating. (3)Depending on your preference, season with salt and pepper. Immediately serve or store in the refrigerator for up to a week with no refrigeration required.

LEMON ENERGY BALLS

Total Time: 15 minutes | Prep Time: 15 minutes

Ingredients:

1 cup rolled oats

1/2 cup cashews

1(about one lemon) a quarter cup of lemon juice

1/4 cup honey or maple syrup

1/4 cup desiccated coconut

1 tsp lemon zest

Directions:

(1) Sun-dried tomatoes, walnuts, basil, and garlic should be mixed together in a food processor. Pulse until the mixture is coarsely minced. **(2)** To achieve the proper consistency of the dip, gradually include the olive oil while the processor is operating. **(3)** Depending on your preference, season with salt and pepper. Immediately serve or store in the refrigerator for up to a week with no refrigeration required.

PUMPKIN SPICE MACAROONS

Total Time: 30 minutes | Prep Time: 15 minutes

Ingredients:

1 1/2 cups shredded coconut	1/2 cup pumpkin puree
1/4 cup honey or maple syrup	1/2 tsp ground cinnamon
1/4 tsp ground nutmeg	1/4 tsp ground ginger
1/4 tsp salt	

Directions:

(1) Get your oven ready for 350 degrees Fahrenheit (175 degrees Celsius) by lining a baking sheet with parchment paper. **(2)** The shredded coconut, pumpkin puree, honey (or maple syrup), cinnamon, nutmeg, ginger, and salt should be well mixed together in a food processor until they are completely incorporated. **(3)** Place the mixture in small mounds onto the baking sheet that has been prepared by using a cookie scoop or a spoon of a similar size. **(4)** Bake the edges for fifteen minutes or until they have a golden brown color. Wait until the dish has completely cooled before serving.

HOMEMADE NUT BUTTER

Total Time: 10 minutes | Prep Time: 10 minutes

Ingredients:

2 cups nuts (almonds, cashews, peanuts, etc.)	1/2 tsp salt
1-2 tbsp oil (if needed, depending on the nuts)	

Directions:

(1) Put the nuts in a food processor and process them. The nuts should be processed for around five minutes, with the sides being scraped down as necessary until they become a smooth butter. **(2)** Put in the salt, then mix everything together. **(3)** You may need to add a little oil to the butter in order to achieve the proper consistency if it is too thick. You may keep it in the refrigerator for up to a month if you store it in an airtight container.

GREEK TZATZIKI

Total Time: 10 minutes | Prep Time: 10 minutes

Ingredients:

1 cup Greek yogurt	1/2 cucumber, grated, and excess moisture squeezed out
2 cloves garlic, minced	1 tbsp fresh dill, chopped
1 tbsp olive oil	1 tbsp lemon juice
Salt and pepper to taste	

Directions:

(1) Greek yogurt, grated cucumber, garlic, dill, olive oil, and lemon juice should be the ingredients that are combined in a food processor. Maintain a smooth consistency. **(2)** Add pepper and salt to taste, and season with salt when you are done. **(3)** To ensure that the flavors are able to come together, place the dish in the refrigerator for at least an hour before serving.

STRAWBERRY MACAROONS

Total Time: 30 minutes | Prep Time: 15 minutes

Ingredients:

- 1 1/2 cups shredded coconut
- 1/4 cup honey or maple syrup
- 1/2 cup fresh strawberries, pureed
- 1/4 tsp salt

Directions:

(1) Get your oven ready for 350 degrees Fahrenheit (175 degrees Celsius) by lining a baking sheet with parchment paper. (2) The shredded coconut, strawberry puree, honey (or maple syrup), and salt should be well mixed together in a food processor until they are completely incorporated. (3) Place the mixture in small mounds onto the baking sheet that has been prepared by using a cookie scoop or a spoon of a similar size. (4) Bake the edges for fifteen minutes or until they have a golden brown color. Wait until the dish has completely cooled before serving.

ALMOND COOKIES

Total Time: 25 minutes | Prep Time: 10 minutes

Ingredients:

- 1 cup almond flour
- 1/4 cup almond butter
- 1/4 tsp salt
- 1/4 cup honey or maple syrup
- 1/2 tsp vanilla extract

Directions:

(1) You should prepare a baking sheet by lining it with parchment paper and then putting it In an oven that is preheated to 175 degrees Celsius (350 degrees Fahrenheit), where the food is placed. (2) Almond flour, honey (or maple syrup), almond butter, vanilla extract, and salt should be mixed together in a food processor until a dough becomes formed. (3) On the baking sheet that has been prepared, add tablespoon-sized portions of dough and slightly flatten them. (4) Bake for fifteen minutes or until the top is golden brown. Before serving, wait until the dish has totally cooled down.

MACADAMIA ENERGY BALLS

Total Time: 15 minutes | Prep Time: 15 minutes

Ingredients:

- 1 cup rolled oats
- 1/4 cup dried apricots, chopped
- 1/4 cup almond butter
- 1/2 cup macadamia nuts
- 1/4 cup honey or maple syrup
- 1 tsp vanilla extract

Directions:

(1) Combine the oats and macadamia nuts in a food processor and process until the mixture is very finely minced. (2) The dried apricots, honey (or maple syrup), almond butter, and vanilla essence should be added to the mixture. The mixture should be processed until it becomes cohesive. (3) Create balls with a diameter of approximately one inch using the mixture. (4) You may keep it in the refrigerator for up to two weeks if you store it in an airtight container.

SMOKY VEGAN CHEESE

Total Time: 10 minutes | Prep Time: 10 minutes

Ingredients:

- 1-2 hours of soaking and draining 1 cup of raw cashews
- 1 tbsp lemon juice
- 1/2 tsp garlic powder
- 1/4 cup nutritional yeast
- 1 tbsp smoked paprika
- Salt to taste

Water, as needed

Directions:

(1)Start a food processor and add the cashews, nutritional yeast, sugar, smoked paprika, garlic powder, and lemon juice. Maintain a smooth consistency. (2)A small amount of water should be added at a time until the proper consistency is achieved. (3)Add salt to taste and season with it. You can serve it right away, or you can put it in the refrigerator for up to seven days.

LEMON HERB BUTTER

Total Time: 10 minutes | Prep Time: 10 minutes

Ingredients:

1 cup unsalted butter, softened	2 tbsp lemon juice
1 tbsp fresh parsley, chopped	1 tbsp fresh chives, chopped
1 tsp lemon zest	Salt to taste

Directions:

(1)Juice the lemon, add the parsley, chives, and butter that has melted, and process until smooth. (2)Taste and add salt as desired. Keep it in the fridge for up to two weeks after transferring it to an airtight container.

RED VELVET MACAROONS

Total Time: 30 minutes | Prep Time: 15 minutes

Ingredients:

1 1/2 cups shredded coconut	1/2 cup beet juice (for color and flavor)
1/4 cup honey or maple syrup	1/4 tsp salt

Directions:

(1)First, prepare your oven to 350 degrees Fahrenheit (175 degrees Celsius). Then, line a baking sheet with parchment paper. (2)To prepare the beetroot juice, shredded coconut, honey (or maple syrup), and salt, use a food processor to cut them into coarse pieces. (3)To prepare the baking sheet, use a tiny spoon or cookie scoop to drop little mounds of the mixture. (4)Just before the sides start to become golden brown, bake for another 15 minutes. Let it cool entirely before you eat it.

APPLE COMPOTE

Total Time: 30 minutes | Prep Time: 10 minutes

Ingredients:

4 large apples, peeled, cored	1/4 cup brown sugar
1/4 cup water	1 tsp cinnamon
1/2 tsp vanilla extract	

Directions:

(1)Chop the apples roughly by adding them to the food processor and pulsing. (2)With the cinnamon, brown sugar, water, and diced apples, bring to a boil in a saucepan set over medium heat. (3)To soften the apples, cook for around fifteen to twenty minutes, stirring once or twice. (4)Cook for an additional two minutes after adding vanilla extract. (5)Let the compote cool down before you dig in. Refrigerate for up to a week if stored in an airtight container.

FALAFEL

Total Time: 45 minutes | Prep Time: 15 minutes

Ingredients:

1 1/2 cups dried chickpeas, soaked overnight and drained
1/2 cup fresh cilantro leaves
3 cloves garlic, peeled
1 tsp ground coriander
Salt and pepper, to taste
1/2 cup fresh parsley leaves
1 small onion, roughly chopped
1 tsp ground cumin
1/2 tsp baking powder
Oil for frying

Directions:

(1)Run the chickpeas through a food processor to make coarse chops. To make a coarse paste, add the parsley, cilantro, garlic, and onion and pulse until combined. (2)Mix in the baking powder, pepper, cumin, coriander, and salt after transferring the batter to a bowl. (3)Make little balls or patties out of the mixture, each about 1 1/2 inches in diameter. (4)Preheat a food processor and pulse the pecans until they reach a fine powder. Brown the falafel in batches in the oil, cooking for approximately three to four minutes on each side. (5)Hot, drained, and accompanied by tahini sauce or pita bread and fresh veggies, serve with a side of paper towels.

STRAWBERRY BANANA SMOOTHIE

Total Time: 5 minutes | Prep Time: 5 minutes

Ingredients:

1 banana, peeled and sliced
1/2 cup plain yogurt
1 tbsp honey (optional)
1 cup fresh or frozen strawberries
1/2 cup milk (dairy or non-dairy)

Directions:

1.Start by putting all of the items into a blender or food processor. (2)Until the mixture is silky smooth and creamy. (3)The drink should be served immediately in a glass, and fresh fruit can be decorated with pleasure.

BANANA COMPOTE

Total Time: 20 minutes | Prep Time: 10 minutes

Ingredients:

4 ripe bananas, sliced
1/4 cup water
1/2 tsp vanilla extract
1/4 cup brown sugar
1/2 tsp ground cinnamon

Directions:

(1)Put the cinnamon, brown sugar, water, and bananas into a saucepan and mix them together. (2)Cook the bananas over medium heat, stirring them occasionally, for around ten to fifteen minutes or until they have become more pliable. (3)Continue to simmer for a further two minutes after adding the vanilla extract. (4)Before serving, remove it from the fire and allow it to cool down.

Coconut Smoothie

Total Time: 5 minutes | Prep Time: 5 minutes

Ingredients:

1 cup coconut milk
1/2 cup pineapple chunks (fresh or frozen)
1 tbsp honey (optional)
1/2 cup coconut water
1/2 cup mango chunks (fresh or frozen)

Directions:

(1)Start by putting all of the items into a blender or food processor. (2)Until the mixture is silky smooth and creamy. (3)Transfer the liquid into a glass and serve it right away.

CARROT SOUP

Total Time: 40 minutes | Prep Time: 10 minutes

Ingredients:

- 1 lb carrots, peeled and chopped
- 3 cloves garlic, peeled
- 1 tbsp olive oil
- Salt and pepper, to taste
- 1 onion, roughly chopped
- 4 cups vegetable broth
- 1 tsp ground ginger

Directions:

(1) Carrots, onion, and garlic should be pulsed in a food processor until they are as finely chopped as possible. (2) Prepare the olive oil by heating it in a big pot over medium heat. Sauté the vegetables for five minutes after adding the chopped vegetables. (3) Toss in the vegetable broth and bring to a boil. The carrots should be cooked at a low simmer for twenty to twenty-five minutes until they are soft. (4) The soup can be pureed until it is completely smooth by using either a food processor or an immersion blender. (5) Ginger, salt, and pepper should be used as seasonings in a hot serving.

VEGGIE BURGERS

Total Time: 30 minutes | Prep Time: 15 minutes

Ingredients:

- 1 can black beans, drained and rinsed
- 1/2 cup breadcrumbs
- 1/2 cup finely chopped bell pepper
- 1 tbsp soy sauce
- 1/2 tsp smoked paprika
- 1/2 cup oats
- 1/2 cup finely chopped onion
- 1 clove garlic, minced
- 1 tsp cumin
- Salt and pepper, to taste
- Oil for frying

Directions:

(1) Use a food processor to pulse the black beans until they resemble mashed potatoes. Then, combine the oats, breadcrumbs, onion, bell pepper, garlic, soy sauce, cumin, smoky paprika, salt, and pepper. (2) Shape into patties the mixture. (3) Grease a skillet and set it over medium heat. When patties are golden brown, cook for four to five minutes per side. (4) Top with anything you choose and place on buns.

RASPBERRY MACAROONS

Total Time: 1 hour | Prep Time: 20 minutes

Ingredients:

- 2 cups shredded coconut
- 1/2 cup condensed milk
- 1/2 cup raspberries
- 1 tsp vanilla extract

Directions:

(1) Before you put the baking sheet in the oven, line it with parchment paper and preheat it to 325°F, or 165°C. (2) Blend the raspberries and coconut together in a food processor until completely smooth. Before you put the baking sheet in the oven, line it with parchment paper and preheat it to 325°F, or 165°C. (3) Blend the raspberries and coconut together in a food processor until completely smooth. After the condensed milk and vanilla essence have been added, process until a combined mixture forms. (4) Onto the baking sheet that has been preheated, spoon large spoonfuls of the mixture. To get a golden brown color, bake for 15 to 20 minutes.

CHOCOLATE HAZELNUT ENERGY BALLS

Total Time: 15 minutes | Prep Time: 10 minutes

Ingredients:

1 cup hazelnuts
1/4 cup cocoa powder
1 tbsp coconut oil
1 cup dates, pitted
1 tbsp honey

Directions:

(1) Process the hazelnuts in a food processor until they are finely minced. (2) Once the dates, cocoa powder, honey, and coconut oil are added, pulse the mixture until mixed thoroughly. (3) Put it in the fridge for at least half an hour after shaping it into little balls.

CHOCOLATE CHIP ENERGY BALLS

Total Time: 15 minutes | Prep Time: 10 minutes

Ingredients:

1 cup rolled oats
1/4 cup honey
1/4 cup ground flaxseed
1/2 cup peanut butter
1/4 cup chocolate chips

Directions:

(1) Ground flaxseed, peanut butter, honey, chocolate chips, and oats should all be mixed together in a food processor. (2) Blend until combined. (3) Before serving, chill for 30 minutes after rolling into balls.

AVOCADO SMOOTHIE

Total Time: 5 minutes | Prep Time: 5 minutes

Ingredients:

1 ripe avocado
1 cup spinach leaves
1 banana
1 tbsp honey (optional)
1 cup almond milk

Directions:

(1) All of the ingredients should be placed in a blender or food processor. (2) Blend until it is completely smooth. (3) You should serve it right away in a glass.

OAT MILK YOGURT

Total Time: 12 hours | Prep Time: 10 minutes

Ingredients:

1 cup rolled oats
1 probiotic capsule
3 cups water

Directions:

(1) Make sure the oats and water are totally smooth by processing them in a food processor. (2) After pouring into a jar, mix with the probiotic powder that was contained in the capsule. (3) Fermentation should be allowed to take place at room temperature for a period of twelve hours with the lid on. (4) The dish should be refrigerated and enjoyed with granola or fresh fruit.

PEANUT BUTTER COOKIES

Total Time: 30 minutes | Prep Time: 10 minutes

Ingredients:

1 cup peanut butter
1 egg
1/2 cup sugar
1/2 tsp baking powder

Directions:

(1) Turn the oven on to 175 degrees Celsius (350 degrees Fahrenheit) and bake until the top is browned. (2) Put all of the ingredients into a food

processor and pulse them until they are completely smooth. **(3)**After pressing the mixture with a fork, form before placing them on a baking pan. Roll into balls. **(4)**Cook for 10–12 minutes or until golden on top. Let cool completely before enjoying.

APPLE CINNAMON OATMEAL

Total Time: 10 minutes | Prep Time: 5 minutes

Ingredients:

1 cup rolled oats	1 apple, peeled, cored, and chopped
1 cup milk or plant-based milk	1/2 teaspoon ground cinnamon
1 tablespoon honey or maple syrup	A pinch of salt
1/4 cup chopped nuts (optional)	

Directions:

(1) The rolled oats should be placed in a food processor and pulsed until they are chopped into a fine consistency. **(2)**In a pot, combine the cubed oats with the milk, apple, cinnamon, honey or maple syrup, and salt. **(3)**When the oats are soft and the mixture has thickened about five minutes, simmer the mixture over medium heat, stirring regularly, until thoroughly combined. **(4)**It should be transferred to a bowl, and if desired, nuts should be sprinkled on top.

CHOCOLATE YOGURT

Total Time: 5 minutes | Prep Time: 5 minutes

Ingredients:

1 cup plain Greek yogurt	2 tablespoons cocoa powder
1 tablespoon honey or maple syrup	1/2 teaspoon vanilla extract
1 tablespoon dark chocolate chips (optional)	

Directions:

(1) Using a blender, combine the yogurt, cocoa powder, honey or maple syrup, and vanilla extract. Blend the mixture until it is fully smooth. This will result in a smooth concoction. **(2)**Keep running the machine until everything is combined and smooth. **(3)**Place the mixture in dishes, and if you so choose, garnish with dark chocolate chips. **(4)**Immediately serve or store in the refrigerator until you are ready to serve.

MANGO COMPOTE

Total Time: 20 minutes | Prep Time: 10 minutes

Ingredients:

2 ripe mangoes, peeled, pitted, and diced	1/4 cup water
2 tablespoons sugar or honey	1 tablespoon lemon juice
1/4 teaspoon ground ginger (optional)	

Directions:

(1) Place the sliced mangoes in a food processor and pulse them until they have a slight chunkiness to them. **(2)**The mango puree, water, sugar or honey, lemon juice, and ginger should be mixed together in a saucepan of medium intensity. **(3)**During the approximately ten minutes that the ingredients are cooking over medium heat, stir them every so often. This should be done until the sauce reaches the desired consistency. **(4)**Prior to serving, allow the dish to cool. This can be kept in the refrigerator for up to a week if it is stored in an airtight container.

BUFFALO CHICKEN DIP

Total Time: 30 minutes | Prep Time: 10 minutes

Ingredients:

- 2 cups cooked chicken, shredded
- 1/2 cup hot sauce (e.g., Frank's RedHot)
- 1/2 cup shredded cheddar cheese
- 8 oz cream cheese, softened
- 1/2 cup ranch dressing
- 1/4 cup chopped green onions

Directions:

(1)Combine the cream cheese, spicy sauce, and ranch dressing in a food processor and process until the mixture is completely smooth. (2)The shredded chicken should be added and pulsed until it is mixed but still has some chunks. (3)Place the mixture in a dish that can be baked in the oven, and then sprinkle the top with shredded cheddar cheese. (4)Put in the oven and cook until the mixture bubbles, about 20 minutes at 350°F (175°C). (5)As a garnish, sprinkle some chopped green onions on top, and serve the dish hot with crackers, chips, or vegetables.

SWEET POTATO HUMMUS

Total Time: 15 minutes | Prep Time: 10 minutes

Ingredients:

- 1 cup cooked sweet potato, mashed
- 1/4 cup tahini
- 2 cloves garlic
- 1 teaspoon ground cumin
- 1 can (15 oz) chickpeas, drained
- 2 tablespoons olive oil
- 2 tablespoons lemon juice
- Salt and pepper to taste

Directions:

(1)Put the chickpeas, sweet potato, tahini, olive oil, garlic, lemon juice, cumin, salt, and pepper into a food processor and pulse until everything is just combined. (2)Blend until smooth, paying attention to the sides of the bowl as necessary. (3)Pita bread, crackers, or fresh veggies can be served alongside this dish. Put in the refrigerator for up to five days before serving.

PISTACHIO MACAROONS

Total Time: 25 minutes | Prep Time: 10 minutes

Ingredients:

- 1 1/2 cups unsweetened shredded coconut
- 1/4 cup honey or maple syrup
- 2 egg whites
- 1/2 cup pistachios, shelled
- 1 teaspoon vanilla extract
- A pinch of salt

Directions:

(1)Preheat the oven to 175 degrees Celsius (350 degrees Fahrenheit). In order to get a baking pan ready, first line it with parchment paper and then set it away separately. (2)Pulse the pistachios in a food processor until they are broken up into very small pieces. (3)The shredded coconut, honey or maple syrup, vanilla essence, egg whites, and salt should be added to the coconut mixture. Pulse until all is incorporated. (4)Transfer chunks of the size of a tablespoon onto the parchment paper that has been prepped for baking. (5)In order to get a color that is golden brown, bake for twelve to fifteen minutes. Prior to serving, allow the dish to cool.

CHOCOLATE SMOOTHIE

Total Time: 5 minutes | Prep Time: 5 minutes

Ingredients:

- 1 banana, frozen
- 1 tablespoon cocoa powder
- 1 tablespoon honey or maple syrup
- 1 cup milk or plant-based milk
- 1 tablespoon almond butter
- 1/2 teaspoon vanilla extract

Directions:

(1)The ingredients should be mixed together in a food processor or blender and then blended until they are completely smooth and creamy. (2)The mixture should then be poured into a glass and served immediately.

SWEET CORN SOUP

Total Time: 20 minutes | Prep Time: 10 minutes

Ingredients:

- 2 cups fresh or frozen corn kernels
- 1 garlic clove, minced
- 1/2 cup coconut milk
- 2 tablespoons olive oil
- 1 onion, chopped
- 2 cups vegetable broth
- Salt and pepper to taste

Directions:

(1)To prepare the olive oil, heat it in a big saucepan until it reaches a temperature of medium. Onion and garlic should be sautéed until they become tender. (2)In addition, sauté the corn kernels for an additional five minutes. (3)Add the vegetable broth, then bring the mixture to a boil. Put the heat down and let it simmer for ten minutes. (4)Simply place the mixture in a food processor and pulse it until it is completely smooth. (5)You should then return the mixture to the stove, stir in the coconut milk, and bring the mixture to a boil. Use pepper and salt to season the food. (6)Serve when still heated.

COCONUT CHOCOLATE MACAROONS

Total Time: 30 minutes | Prep Time: 15 minutes

Ingredients:

- 1 1/2 cups shredded coconut
- 1/2 cup dark chocolate chips, melted
- A pinch of salt
- 1/2 cup sweetened condensed milk
- 1 teaspoon vanilla extract

Directions:

(1)Set oven temperature to 350°F, or 175°C. Put parchment paper on a baking pan. (2)Shredded coconut, sweetened condensed milk, vanilla essence, and salt should all be mixed together in a food processor. Mix by pulsing. (3)Bake for 15 to 20 minutes, or until a golden brown color has developed, after dropping spoonfuls onto the baking sheet. (4)Before serving, let cool and top with melted chocolate.

MACADAMIA NUT MILK YOGURT

Total Time: 10 minutes (plus chilling time) | Prep Time: 10 minutes

Ingredients:

- 1 cup macadamia nuts, soaked overnight
- 2 tablespoons plain yogurt (as a starter culture)
- 2 cups water
- 1 tablespoon maple syrup (optional)

Directions:

(1)Rinse and drain the macadamia nuts. Mix the nuts and water in a food processor and pulse until smooth. (2)After transferring to a bowl, mix in the maple syrup and yogurt. (3)The fermentation process takes around 6-8 hours at room temperature, so cover with a towel and set aside. (4)Put it in the fridge and let it chill for at least two hours before you serve it.

TAHINI ENERGY BALLS

Total Time: 10 minutes | Prep Time: 10 minutes

Ingredients:

1 cup rolled oats
1/4 cup honey or maple syrup
1/4 cup chia seeds
1/2 cup tahini
1/4 cup chocolate chips
1 teaspoon vanilla extract

Directions:

The following ingredients should be combined in a food processor: oats, tahini, honey/maple syrup, chocolate chips, chia seeds, and vanilla. A sticky dough will be formed after pulsing. Before placing on a parchment-lined baking sheet, roll into little balls. Put it in the fridge for half an hour before you eat it. Put in the refrigerator in a sealed container.

SPINACH SMOOTHIE

Total Time: 5 minutes | Prep Time: 5 minutes

Ingredients:

1 cup fresh spinach
1/2 cup unsweetened almond milk
1 tablespoon chia seeds
1/2 cup ice cubes
1 banana
1/4 cup Greek yogurt
1 tablespoon honey or maple syrup (optional)

Directions:

(1)In a food processor, combine the banana, almond milk, spinach, Greek yogurt, chia seeds, and honey or maple syrup (if using). (2)Combine ingredients and mix until creamy. (3)Blend in the ice cubes until smooth, then repeat if necessary. (4)Fill a glass with it and savor it right away.

BIRTHDAY CAKE ENERGY BALLS

Total Time: 15 minutes | Prep Time: 15 minutes

Ingredients:

1 cup rolled oats
1/4 cup cashew butter
2 tablespoons vanilla protein powder
1 teaspoon vanilla extract
1/2 cup almond flour
1/4 cup maple syrup
2 tablespoons rainbow sprinkles
Pinch of salt

Directions:

(1)Put the rolled oats in a food processor and pulse them until they are completely pulverized. (2)Add almond flour, cashew butter, maple syrup, protein powder, vanilla extract, and salt. Process until a dough forms. (3)Add rainbow sprinkles and pulse a few times to combine. (4)One tablespoon of dough should be scooped out and then rolled into balls. For the remaining mixture, repeat the process. (5)Place it in an airtight jar and place it in the refrigerator for up to a week.

TOMATO SOUP

Total Time: 30 minutes | Prep Time: 10 minutes

Ingredients:

1 tablespoon olive oil
1 medium onion, chopped

3 cloves garlic, minced

1 cup vegetable broth

1 teaspoon dried oregano

1/4 cup heavy cream (optional)

2 cans (14.5 oz each) diced tomatoes

1 teaspoon dried basil

Salt and pepper to taste

Directions:

(1)To preheat the olive oil, place it in a pot and set the heat to medium. Bring the garlic and onion to a gentle boil. (2)Put the chopped tomatoes and onion mixture in a food processor. Whip till completely smooth. (3)After whisking, return to the saucepan and stir in the vegetable stock, oregano, basil, salt, and pepper. (4)After the mixture boils, lower the heat and simmer for twenty minutes. (5)Toss in heavy cream, if desired, and enjoy while still hot.

VEGAN BLUE CHEESE

Total Time: 2 hours (including chilling) | Prep Time: 10 minutes

Ingredients:

Cashews, uncooked, soaking for two to four hours, one cup

2 tablespoons nutritional yeast

1 tablespoon lemon juice

1/4 teaspoon garlic powder

1/4 cup water

1 tablespoon apple cider vinegar

1/2 teaspoon salt

1 tablespoon spirulina powder (for the "blue" veins)

Directions:

(1)In a food processor, the cashews, water, nutritional yeast, vinegar, lemon juice, salt, and garlic powder should be combined and processed until they are completely incorporated. (2)Place half of the mixture in a separate bowl. (3)Pulse the remaining ingredients in the machine a few times to incorporate the spirulina powder. (4)To make it seem marbled, layer the plain mixture on top of the spirulina mixture in a bowl or cheese mold in alternate layers. (5)Put in the fridge for at least two hours before you serve.

PEANUT BUTTER YOGURT

Total Time: 5 minutes | Prep Time: 5 minutes

Ingredients:

1 cup Greek yogurt

1 tablespoon honey or maple syrup

Toppings: granola, fruit, or nuts

2 tablespoons natural peanut butter

1/2 teaspoon vanilla extract

Directions:

(1)In a food processor, combine peanut butter, Greek yogurt, honey, and vanilla extract until it's completely smooth. (2)To garnish, you can use granola, fruit, or nuts. Pour into a bowl and serve.

TOFU CREAM CHEESE

Total Time: 10 minutes | Prep Time: 10 minutes

Ingredients:

1 block (14 oz) firm tofu, drained and pressed

2 tablespoons lemon juice

1 tablespoon olive oil

1/4 teaspoon garlic powder

2 tablespoons nutritional yeast

1 tablespoon apple cider vinegar

1/2 teaspoon salt

1 tablespoon fresh herbs (optional)

Directions:

84 | Page

(1)Combine all of the ingredients in a food processor and process them until they are completely incorporated. (2)Taste and adjust seasoning to taste. Incorporate fresh herbs, if desired. (3)Refrigerate for up to five days if stored in an airtight container.

APRICOT COMPOTE

Total Time: 15 minutes | Prep Time: 5 minutes

Ingredients:

1 cup dried apricots
1 tablespoon lemon juice
1/2 cup water
1 tablespoon honey or sugar

Directions:

(1)Pulse the dried apricots in a food processor until they are finely minced. (2)The apricots, water, lemon juice, and honey/sugar should be combined in a pot. (3)Cook, stirring occasionally, for 10 minutes at a simmer. (4)Chill before you eat. Keep in the refrigerator for a maximum of two weeks.

MOCHA MACAROONS

Total Time: 30 minutes | Prep Time: 15 minutes

Ingredients:

1 1/2 cups unsweetened shredded coconut
1/4 cup cocoa powder
1 tablespoon brewed coffee
Pinch of salt
1/2 cup almond flour
1/4 cup maple syrup
1 teaspoon vanilla extract

Directions:

(1)Preheat the oven to 325 degrees Fahrenheit, which is 160 degrees Celsius. Put parchment paper on a baking pan. (2)After the condensed milk and vanilla essence have been added, process until a combined mixture forms. (3)To make balls, scoop out a tablespoon of the mixture. Lay out on a baking pan. (4)After 15 minutes in the oven, you should see some golden edges. (5)Permit to cool completely before consumption.

HOMEMADE REFRIED BEANS

Total Time: 15 minutes | Prep Time: 5 minutes

Ingredients:

2 cups cooked pinto beans
2 cloves garlic, minced
1 teaspoon ground cumin
1/4 cup vegetable broth
1/4 cup onion, chopped
1 tablespoon olive oil
Salt and pepper to taste

Directions:

(1)The beans, garlic, onion, cumin, olive oil, salt, and pepper should be blended together in a food processor. (2)To adjust the consistency, cook the mixture for around five minutes in a skillet over medium heat, adding vegetable broth as required during the cooking process. Required during the cooking process. (3)Warm it up and use it as a side dish or filler.

LEMON POPPY SEED MACAROONS

Total Time: 25 minutes | Prep Time: 10 minutes

Ingredients:

1 1/2 cups shredded coconut
1/4 cup maple syrup
1/2 cup almond flour
1 tablespoon lemon juice

Zest of 1 lemon

1 tablespoon poppy seeds

Directions:

(1) Before you begin, bring the oven temperature up to 325 °F or 160 °C. Put parchment paper on a baking pan. (2) Put all of the ingredients into a food processor and pulse them until they are thoroughly combined. (3) To make balls, scoop out a tablespoon of the mixture. Lay out on a baking pan. (4) Brown the top of the dish after 15 minutes in the oven. Chill before you eat.

FRESH TOMATO SAUCE

Total Time: 30 minutes | Prep Time: 10 minutes

Ingredients:

4 large ripe tomatoes
2 cloves garlic, minced
1 teaspoon dried oregano
1/4 cup fresh basil, chopped
1/2 cup onion, chopped
1 tablespoon olive oil
Salt and pepper to taste

Directions:

(1) A food processor should be used to combine the tomatoes, garlic, and onion. (2) To warm the olive oil, place it in a saucepan and set the heat to medium. Garnish with oregano, salt, pepper, and the tomato mixture. (3) Stir occasionally as it simmers for 20 minutes. (4) Toss up some fresh basil and enjoy with spaghetti or any other way you like.

PINEAPPLE COMPOTE

Total Time: 20 minutes | Prep Time: 5 minutes

Ingredients:

2 cups fresh pineapple chunks
1/4 cup water
1/4 cup sugar
1 tablespoon lemon juice

Directions:

(1) Chop the pineapple finely in a food processor. (2) The pineapple, sugar, water, and lemon juice should all be combined in a pot first. (3) Maintain a simmer while whisking the mixture on occasion for fifteen minutes or until it reaches the desired consistency. (4) Permit to cool completely before consumption. Keep in the refrigerator for a maximum of one week.

RASPBERRY VANILLA SPREAD

Total Time: 10 minutes | Prep Time: 5 minutes

Ingredients:

1 cup fresh raspberries
1 teaspoon vanilla extract
1/4 cup honey or maple syrup
1 tablespoon chia seeds

Directions:

(1) Put honey, vanilla essence, and raspberries into a food processor and mix until smooth. Blend until it is completely smooth. (2) Mix in the

PUMPKIN SEED CHEESE

Total Time: 15 minutes | Prep Time: 10 minutes

Ingredients:

1 cup pumpkin seeds, soaked overnight
1 tbsp apple cider vinegar
1 garlic clove
2 tbsp nutritional yeast
1 tbsp lemon juice
1/2 tsp salt

1/4 cup water (or as needed)

Directions:

(1)After soaking the pumpkin seeds, drain and rinse them. (2)In a food processor, combine the seeds, nutritional yeast, olive oil, lemon zest, salt, and apple cider vinegar. (3)Add water little by little while blending until the mixture is smooth and creamy, then spreadable. (4)Reevaluate the seasoning according to your taste. (5)Refrigerate for up to seven days if stored in an airtight container.

WALNUT BUTTER

Total Time: 10 minutes | Prep Time: 5 minutes

Ingredients:

2 cups walnuts
1-2 tbsp maple syrup (optional)
Pinch of salt

Directions:

(1)Add walnuts to the food processor. (2)Process for 5-10 minutes, scraping down the sides as needed, until the walnuts break down and turn into a smooth butter. (3)Add maple syrup and salt to taste, and process again until fully combined. (4)To keep it fresh for up to a month, transfer it to a jar and put it in the refrigerator.

CHICKPEA BURGERS

Total Time: 30 minutes | Prep Time: 15 minutes

Ingredients:

1 can chickpeas, drained and rinsed
1/2 cup rolled oats
1/4 cup onion, chopped
2 garlic cloves
1 tbsp tahini
1 tsp cumin
Olive oil (for frying)
1 tbsp lemon juice
Salt and pepper to taste

Directions:

(1)Using a food processor, combine the following Ingredients: chickpeas, oats, onion, garlic, tahini, lemon juice, cumin, salt, and pepper. (2)Pulse until everything is thoroughly blended yet contains some chunks. (3)The ingredients should be formed into patties. (4)A small amount of olive oil should be heated in a pan over medium heat. To get a golden brown color, cook the patties for approximately four to five minutes on each side. (5)Buns, lettuce, tomato, and the sauce of your choice should be served alongside.

VEGAN PANEER

Total Time: 40 minutes | Prep Time: 15 minutes

Ingredients:

1 cup cashews, soaked for 4 hours
2 tbsp nutritional yeast
1 tbsp lemon juice
1 tsp apple cider vinegar
1/2 tsp salt
1/2 cup water

Directions:

(1)After the cashews have been soaked, drain them and then add them to the food processor. (2)The following ingredients should be added: water, lemon juice, apple cider vinegar, nutritional yeast, and salt. (3)To achieve a smooth and creamy consistency, process. (4)In order to firm up the mixture, pour it into a mold that has been lined with cheesecloth and place it in the refrigerator for at least two hours. (5)To use in salads or curries, cut into cubes and dice.

TAHINI CHEESE

Total Time: 20 minutes | Prep Time: 10 minutes

Ingredients:

- 1/2 cup tahini
- 1 tbsp lemon juice
- 1 garlic clove
- 1/4 cup nutritional yeast
- 1 tbsp miso paste
- 1/4 cup water

Directions:

(1) Place everything in a food processor. (2) To make it spreadable, add more water if necessary and blend until smooth. (3) See if the seasoning needs adjusting by tasting. (4) Put in a sealed jar and refrigerate for no more than a week.

ALMOND RICOTTA

Total Time: 15 minutes | Prep Time: 10 minutes

Ingredients:

- 1 cup almonds, soaked overnight
- 1 tbsp lemon juice
- 1/4 tsp salt
- 1 tbsp nutritional yeast
- 1 garlic clove
- 1/4 cup water (or as needed)

Directions:

(1) Before rinsing, drain the soaked almonds. (2) Almonds, nutritional yeast, garlic, lemon juice, and salt should be made into a mixture in a food processor. (3) The mixture should be mixed until it is completely incorporated, and water should be added gradually until it achieves the desired combination consistency. (4) See if the seasoning needs adjusting by tasting. (5) Put it in the fridge and keep it for up to seven days.

ALMOND FLOUR PANCAKES

Total Time: 20 minutes | Prep Time: 10 minutes

Ingredients:

- 1 cup almond flour
- 1/2 cup almond milk
- 1 tsp baking powder
- 1 tbsp flaxseed meal
- 1 tsp vanilla extract
- Pinch of salt

Directions:

(1) All of the ingredients should be combined and processed in a food processor until they are completely incorporated. (2) On medium heat, warm a nonstick skillet. (3) Cook for two to three minutes per side, or until golden brown, after pouring 1/4 cup of batter into the pan. (4) Accompany with maple syrup, seasonal fruit, or other toppings of your choice.

LEMON POPPY SEED ENERGY BALLS

Total Time: 10 minutes | Prep Time: 5 minute

Ingredients:

- 1 cup almonds
- 1 tbsp lemon zest
- 1 tbsp poppy seeds
- 1/2 cup dates, pitted
- 1 tbsp lemon juice

Directions:

(1) A food processor should be used to incorporate the dates and almonds, and then the mixture should be pulsed until it is finely crushed. (2) While pulsing, add poppy seeds, lemon juice, and zest. (3) Make balls out of the mixture and refrigerate for up to a week if sealed properly.

EASY FALAFEL

Total Time: 25 minutes | Prep Time: 10 minutes

Ingredients:

1 cup canned chickpeas,   1/2 cup fresh parsley

drained
1/2 cup fresh cilantro
2 garlic cloves
1 tsp coriander
2 tbsp chickpea flour

1/4 cup onion, chopped
1 tsp cumin
Salt and pepper to taste
Oil for frying

Directions:

(1) Put all of the ingredients, with the exception of the oil and chickpea flour, into a food processor and pulse them until they are combined but still seem chunky. (2) Before shaping into balls, stir in the chickpea flour. (3) Fry the falafel in oil over medium heat until it turns golden brown on all sides. (4) As a side, you can have pita, hummus, and some fresh veggies.

COOKIES AND CREAM MACAROONS

Total Time: 45 minutes | Prep Time: 20 minutes

Ingredients:

2 cups shredded coconut
1 cup crushed chocolate sandwich cookies (e.g., Oreos)
Pinch of salt

1 cup sweetened condensed milk
1 tsp vanilla extract

Directions:

(1) The oven should be preheated to 325 degrees Fahrenheit (165 degrees Celsius), and a baking sheet should be prepared by lining it with parchment paper. Finally, the oven should be prepared. (2) Shredded coconut, sweetened condensed milk, smashed cookies, vanilla essence, and salt should all be mixed together in a food processor. Mix until thoroughly combined and slightly gritty. (3) Create mounds on the prepared baking sheet by scooping portions of the mixture. (4) Brown the edges in the oven for around fifteen to twenty minutes. (5) Before serving, let the macaroons cool entirely on a wire rack.

SALTED CARAMEL ENERGY BALLS

Total Time: 20 minutes | Prep Time: 10 minutes

Ingredients:

1 cup pitted dates
1/2 cup almond butter
1/4 cup honey or maple syrup
1/2 tsp vanilla extract

1 cup rolled oats
1/4 cup unsweetened shredded coconut
1/2 tsp sea salt

Directions:

(1) The following ingredients should be thrown together in order to produce the dough: dates, oats, almond butter, shredded coconut, honey (or maple syrup), sea salt, and vanilla essence. (2) Roll the dough into 1-inch balls and set them on a parchment-lined tray. Chill for at least 10 minutes before you eat them.

MANGO MACAROONS

Total Time: 40 minutes | Prep Time: 15 minutes

Ingredients:

2 cups shredded coconut
1/2 cup sweetened condensed milk

1 cup diced dried mango
1 tsp vanilla extract

Directions:

(1) Before beginning, prepare a baking sheet by lining it with parchment paper and preheating the

oven to 325 degrees Fahrenheit (165 degrees Celsius). Before beginning, prepare a baking sheet by lining it with parchment paper and preheating the oven to 325 degrees Fahrenheit (165 degrees Celsius). (2)Get the shredded coconut, dried mango chunks, sweetened condensed milk, and vanilla essence all mixed up in a food processor. (3)Make little mounds with the mixture by scooping tablespoons onto the baking sheet that has been prepared. (4)Brown the top by baking it for around fifteen to twenty minutes. (5)After baking, set the macaroons on a wire rack to cool.

VEGETABLE DIP

Total Time: 10 minutes | Prep Time: 10 minutes

Ingredients:

1 cup Greek yogurt	1/2 cup sour cream
1/4 cup chopped fresh herbs (e.g., dill, chives, parsley)	1 clove garlic, minced
1 tbsp lemon juice	Salt and pepper to taste

Directions:

(1)Blend together sour cream, Greek yogurt, fresh herbs, garlic powder, lemon juice, and chopped garlic in a food processor. (2)Blend all ingredients until smooth. (3)To taste, season with salt and pepper, depending on your preferences. (4)Accompany with a side of crisp veggies or pita chips..

CLASSIC SALSA

Total Time: 15 minutes | Prep Time: 10 minutes

Ingredients:

4 ripe tomatoes, quartered	1 small onion, quartered
1 jalapeño pepper, seeded (adjust to taste)	2 cloves garlic
1/4 cup fresh cilantro	1 tbsp lime juice
Salt to taste	

Directions:

(1)Put the tomatoes, onion, jalapeño pepper, garlic, and cilantro in a food processor. Pulse until the salsa gets the texture you want (chunky or smooth). (2)Then, add lime juice and salt according to your taste, and pulse once more to incorporate. Chill the salsa before serving to allow the flavors to blend.

BUTTERNUT SQUASH SOUP

Total Time: 1 hour | Prep Time: 15 minutes

Ingredients:

1 butternut squash, peeled, seeded, and cubed when it is of medium size	1 onion, chopped
2 cloves garlic, minced	1 carrot, peeled and chopped
4 cups vegetable or chicken broth	1/2 cup coconut milk
1 tbsp olive oil	1/2 tsp ground cumin
Salt and pepper to taste	

Directions:

(1)Slowly bring olive oil to a simmer in a big saucepan. Once the carrots, onion, and garlic have softened, add them to the sauté pan. (2)Put the butternut squash and the broth in the pot just before it boils. Cover and simmer for twenty to twenty-five minutes or until the squash reaches the desired softness. (3)Puree the soup in portions using a food processor. Go back to the pot. (4)Add coconut milk, cumin, salt, and pepper, and stir to combine. Bring to a boil, then add seasoning and cook until done. (5)Heat and serve immediately.

PISTACHIO SPREAD

Total Time: 10 minutes | Prep Time: 10 minutes

Ingredients:

1 cup shelled pistachios
2 tbsp coconut oil or olive oil
1/2 tsp vanilla extract (optional)
2 tbsp honey
1/4 tsp sea salt

Directions:

(1) Process the pistachios in a food processor until they reach a creamy consistency. (2) Incorporate honey, coconut (or olive) oil, sea salt, and, if desired, vanilla essence. (3) Blend the spread until it's completely smooth. (4) Keep in the fridge for up to two weeks if sealed tightly.

THE END

Printed in Great Britain
by Amazon